MW01716888

The Christian's Job Description

Living Out Faith With Purpose

by
Elaine Jordan

ONE STONE
BIBLICAL RESOURCES

Published by:
One Stone Press
979 Lovers Lane
Bowling Green, KY 42103

Printed in the United States of America

ISBN: 978-1-966992-10-3

ONE STONE
BIBLICAL RESOURCES
1(800)428-0121
www.onestone.com

CONTENTS

Christian Job Description
Entry-level / Mid-level / Senior-level

Christian (Entry, Mid, Senior Level) follows Jesus Christ and demonstrates their love of God with obedience to the gospel. Entry-level, mid-level, and senior positions are available, with room for growth at all levels. This person works in God's kingdom and is an example for other Christians and persons who have not yet accepted the position. Must have or be able to acquire:

- Knowledge of the riches and depth of God's love (Romans 11:33), the gospel and mystery of Christ (1 Timothy 3:16, Romans 15:14)
- Willingness to speak truth to others (1 Timothy 2:7), grow in the faith (Hebrews 5:11-13)
- Ability to be sensitive to their conscience (1 Corinthians 8:6-13), to grow in love, joy, peace, longsuffering, kindness, goodness, faithfulness, gentleness, and self-control (Galatians 5:22-23), to leave all for Christ and prioritize Him over all else (Luke 14:33), to persevere in the position (Matthew 10:22, Revelation 2:10)

General duties include, but are not limited to, the following:

1 Demonstrate Commitment to a Deep, Personal Love and Reverence for God
2 Possess Strong Belief in and Adherence to the Bible as the Authoritative Word of God
3 Ability to Consistently Show Love and Compassion toward Others, Including Colleagues and Community Members
4 Willingness to Undergo and Affirm the Act of Baptism
5 Active Participation in Regular Public Worship Services and Gatherings
6 Commitment to Maintaining a Personal Devotional Life, Including Prayer and Reflection
7 Able to Apply faith through Tangible Acts of Service and Good Works
8 Preparedness and Ability to Effectively Teach and Share Spiritual Principles
9 Demonstrate Capacity to Promote and Maintain Peaceful Relationships in Diverse Environments.
10 Exemplary Control Over Spoken Communication, Including Respectful, Truthful, and Edifying Speech
11 Strong Discernment and Sound Judgment in Moral, Ethical, and Spiritual Matters
12 Consistent Display of Hope, Personal Holiness, and Moral Integrity in Daily Conduct
13 Flexibility to Perform Additional Responsibilities and Duties as Assigned in Alignment with Faith and Mission

Demonstrate Commitment to a Deep, Personal Love and Reverence for God

> *[37]Jesus said to him, "You shall love the Lord your God with all your heart, with all your soul, and with all your mind. [38]This is the first and great commandment," (Matthew 22:37-38).*

Starting this lesson about loving God, as found in Matthew 22:37-38, is effortless, easy-peasy, and obvious. It is like throwing down the biggest trump in a card game with a flourish. However, just knowing God is not playing the trump card to win the game of life. Loving the Lord your God is more than believing there is a God. Everyone wants a savior to keep them from hell, but not everyone wants a Lord.

We must understand who God is and why He deserves love to accomplish the goal of this verse. Then loving God with all your heart, soul, and mind means something, and we can fulfill the first and great commandment.

I AM

Moses needed a name to tell the children of Israel who had sent him to save them from Egyptian slavery. ***[14]And God said to Moses, "I AM WHO I AM." And He said, "Thus you shall say to the children of Israel, 'I AM has sent me to you,' " (Exodus 3:14).***

Humans cannot know God's full power and presence, so the English language has three words often used to describe Him: omnipresent, omnipotent, and omniscient. Omnipresent means present everywhere. Omnipotent means all-powerful. Omniscient means knowledge of everything. All three qualities exist in the past, present, and future for I AM and are part of the word meanings when applied to God.

> *[15]For thus says the High and Lofty One Who inhabits eternity, whose name is Holy... (Isaiah 57:15).*

Omnipresent God is everywhere and in everything, always has been, and always will be. He is not confined to one body, bound by space and time.

Omnipotent God does not rely on anything else to do what He has chosen. Genesis 1 tells us God created the heavens and the earth in the beginning. That is our earthly beginning, not God's beginning. Omnipotent God made all His creation and saw it was good without laboratories, warehouses, and engineers. He spoke the universe and all it contains into existence without requiring anything or anyone else. I AM has boundless power to do whatever He chooses with complete control of this power.

The omniscient God knows everything in the past, present, and future. He makes 100s on all the science tests because He made science. He knows how science works, not just how mankind thinks it works. I AM knows us as individuals. He knew Adam and Eve had sinned (Genesis 3), knew Cain killed Abel (Genesis 4), and personally knows us too. Jeremiah 1:5 teaches us that God knows us before we are born. God knows everything because He created knowledge!

> *"Before I formed you in the womb I knew you; Before you were born I sanctified you; I ordained you a prophet to the nations" (Jeremiah 1:5).*

I AM is omnipresent, omnipotent, and omniscient and commands love and respect with all our minds, souls, and hearts. In Job 38, God reminds Job of His greatness. Read the whole chapter to remind yourself, but the following are a few verses from that chapter to remind the class.

> *[3]Now prepare yourself like a man; I will question you, and you shall answer Me.*
> *[4]"Where were you when I laid the foundations of the earth? Tell Me, if you have*
> *understanding. [5]Who determined its measurements? Surely you know! Or who*
> *stretched the line upon it? [6]To what were its foundations fastened? Or who laid*
> *its cornerstone, [7]When the morning stars sang together, And all the sons of God*
> *shouted for joy [8]"Or who shut in the sea with doors, When it burst forth and*
> *issued from the womb; [9]When I made the clouds its garment, And thick darkness*
> *its swaddling band; [10]When I fixed My limit for it, And set bars and doors; [11]When*
> *I said, 'This far you may come, but no farther, And here your proud waves must*
> *stop!' (Job 38:3-11).*

God's Character Revealed in Psalms

We learn a lot about the character of God in all the Psalms, but let's look at Psalm 18 specifically for an example. In your Bible, highlight phrases describing God in yellow. Below are only the first three verses!

> *[1]I will love You, O Lord, my strength. [2]The Lord is my rock and my fortress and my*
> *deliverer; My God, my strength, in whom I will trust; My shield and the horn of my*
> *salvation, my stronghold. [3]I will call upon the Lord, who is worthy to be praised;*
> *So shall I be saved from my enemies (Psalm 18:1-3).*

This psalm also states the Lord's actions in delivering David from Saul and other enemies. God knew David and the details of his life. God knows us and our lives also.

- God listened to David in his distress.
- God actively delivered David from his enemies.
- God was with David during his hard times and his good times.

Psalm 23 may be the most quoted psalm about God's love and care for His people. God has loved, led, provided for, and protected David in this psalm. God's qualities portrayed to us in only these two psalms describe a powerful, committed, loving, faithful, and caring God who deserves our love and praise. The whole of Psalms only increases the list of God's qualities and other books in the Bible expand on those.

God's Qualities

The Bible reveals God's moral qualities and attributes to us throughout its pages. The following list and thoughts are a sampling of these to discuss our wonderful God who created us.

Holy

As related to God, the word holy means exalted, divine, or worthy of complete devotion as one perfect in purity and righteousness. The word holy, as related to a thing or a person, means venerated or devoted to a deity as a holy temple. As applied to an individual, the word holy means kept separate from earthly temptations and unrighteousness.

> *Exalt the Lord our God, And worship at His holy hill; For the Lord our God is holy (Psalm 99:9).*

Righteous

Righteousness, as applied to God, means morally right, justified, and free from guilt and sin; as applied to mankind, it means acting in accord with God's law.

> *Righteousness and justice are the foundation of Your throne; Mercy and truth go before Your face (Psalm 89:14).*

Merciful and Gracious

Mercy is restraining from inflicting punishment on a law-breaker. God's grace is kindness shown to undeserving individuals and is often described as unmerited favor.

> *4But God, who is rich in mercy, because of His great love with which He loved us,*
> *5even when we were dead in trespasses, made us alive together with Christ (by grace you have been saved) (Ephesians 2:4-5).*

Loving

Love is the feeling of deep affection, care, goodwill, and concern. The Bible teaches us that God not only loves us but is love.

> *8He who does not love does not know God, for God is love. 9In this the love of God was manifested toward us, that God has sent His only begotten Son into the world, that we might live through Him. 10In this is love, not that we loved God, but that He loved us and sent His Son to be the propitiation for our sins (1 John 4:8-10).*

Longsuffering

Longsuffering is being patient during trials and hardships without anger or bitterness, even when provoked. Longsuffering is being patient after the last straw has been reached.

> *Or do you despise the riches of His goodness, forbearance, and longsuffering, not knowing that the goodness of God leads you to repentance (Romans 2:4).*

Forgiving

Forgiveness is giving up any claim for retribution, retaliation, or compensation due to an offense.

> *But You are God, ready to pardon, gracious and merciful, slow to anger, abundant in kindness, and did not forsake them (Nehemiah 9:17b).*

True

In this context, true means the integration of character and adherence to virtue, reliability beyond personal behavior, and the love of truth.

> *[17]Thus God, determining to show more abundantly to the heirs of promise the immutability of His counsel, confirmed it by an oath, [18] that by two immutable things, in which it is impossible for God to lie, we might have strong consolation, who have fled for refuge to lay hold of the hope set before us. [19]This hope we have as an anchor of the soul, both sure and steadfast, and which enters the Presence behind the veil (Hebrews 6:17-19).*

> *I have many things to say and to judge concerning you, but He who sent Me is true; and I speak to the world those things which I heard from Him (John 8:26).*

Faithful

Faithful has an active and passive sense. The active sense means fidelity and trustworthiness. The passive sense means trust and reliance.

> His fidelity to His promises.
> *[3]For what if some did not believe? Will their unbelief make the faithfulness of God without effect? [4]Certainly not! Indeed, let God be true but every man a liar (Romans 3:3-4a).*

> Trust and reliance.
> *God is faithful, by whom you were called into the fellowship of His Son, Jesus Christ our Lord (1 Corinthians 1:9).*

Compassionate

Compassion is a feeling causing acts of mercy and kindness to those who are vulnerable or suffering.

> *Indeed we count them blessed who endure. You have heard of the perseverance of Job and seen the end intended by the Lord—that the Lord is very compassionate and merciful (James 5:11).*

Comforting

Comforting is encouragement in times of need.

> *[3]Blessed be the God and Father of our Lord Jesus Christ, the Father of mercies and God of all comfort, [4]who comforts us in all our tribulation, that we may be able to comfort those who are in any trouble, with the comfort with which we ourselves are comforted by God (2 Corinthians 1:3-4).*

Awesome

Awesome means to inspire wonder, admiration, dread, and reverence. In the following example, the psalmist wants the reader to know God deserves our worship.

He has sent redemption to His people; He has commanded His covenant forever: Holy and awesome is His name (Psalm 111:9).

No Respecter of Persons

God created all people, loves all people, and has chosen to save all people regardless of class, race, or gender.

12For there is no distinction between Jew and Greek, for the same Lord over all is rich to all who call upon Him. 13For "whoever calls on the name of the Lord shall be saved" (Romans 10:12-13).

27For as many of you as were baptized into Christ have put on Christ. 28There is neither Jew nor Greek, there is neither slave nor free, there is neither male nor female; for you are all one in Christ Jesus. 29And if you are Christ's, then you are Abraham's seed, and heirs according to the promise (Galatians 3:27-29).

Vengeful

Vengeance is punishment dealt out for retribution.

As described above, God is loving and merciful; however, He punishes too. The flood, Sodom and Gomorrah, and Achan illustrate how God punishes those who disobey.

O Lord God, to whom vengeance belongs—O God, to whom vengeance belongs, shine forth! (Psalm 94:1).

Beloved, do not avenge yourselves, but rather give place to wrath; for it is written, "Vengeance is Mine, I will repay," says the Lord (Romans 12:19).

Unchanging

God remains the same, the same as He was at creation, the same as today, and the same in the future.

"For I am the Lord, I do not change" (Malachi 3:6a).

But to the Son He says: "Your throne, O God, is forever and ever; A scepter of righteousness is the scepter of Your kingdom" (Hebrews 1:8).

Jesus Christ is the same yesterday, today, and forever (Hebrews 13:8).

Loving God

Psalm 111 is an excellent summary showing that understanding God's greatness leads to reverence of God and obedience to God's commandments. Reverence and obedience are evidence of our love for God.

1Praise the Lord! I will praise the Lord with my whole heart, In the assembly of the upright and in the congregation. 2The works of the Lord are great, Studied by all who have pleasure in them. 3His work is honorable and glorious, And His righteousness endures forever. 4He has made His wonderful works to be re-membered; The Lord is gracious and full of compassion.5 He has given food to those who fear Him; He will ever be mindful of His covenant. 6He has declared to His people the power of His works, In giving them the heritage of the nations.

[7]The works of His hands are verity and justice; All His precepts are sure. [8]They stand fast forever and ever, And are done in truth and uprightness. [9]He has sent redemption to His people; He has commanded His covenant forever: Holy and awesome is His name. [10]The fear of the Lord is the beginning of wisdom; A good understanding have all those who do His commandments. His praise endures forever (Psalm 111:1-10).

God wants all people to love Him with unconditional love and commitment, as is His due. We cannot do this with only an abstract idea of a "Supreme Being." We must know God to love God with all our souls, minds, and hearts.

Our complete love of God must lead to obedience to God. Love and obedience to God go hand in hand and are inseparable.

Therefore you shall love the Lord your God, and keep His charge, His statutes, His judgments, and His commandments always (Deuteronomy 11:1).

By this we know that we love the children of God, when we love God and keep His commandments (1 John 5:2).

Knowing about God without obedience to His precepts is not love for God! Even the demons know God without love and obedience.

They profess to know God, but in works they deny Him, being abominable, disobedient, and disqualified for every good work (Titus 1:16).

Let us alone! What have we to do with You, Jesus of Nazareth? Did You come to destroy us? I know who You are—the Holy One of God (Mark 1:24).

Our love for God is evident when His will has priority over our will or another person's will. God's commandments must come first over any earthly relationship, activity, or group.

No one can serve two masters; for either he will hate the one and love the other, or else he will be loyal to the one and despise the other. You cannot serve God and mammon (Matthew 6:24).

Summary

All people should know who God is and love Him completely. This knowledge and love naturally lead to obedience to God's commandments because the believer knows this is what God wants and deserves. This love and obedience will fulfill the first and great commandment stated in Matthew 22:37-38.

Discussion Questions

1. How would you explain God's omnipresent, omnipotent, and omniscient characteristics to an unbeliever? To a child?

2. How does Psalm 18 apply to us and our relationship with God?

3. Which of God's attributes is the hardest for you to understand?

4. Which of God's attributes do you depend on the most?

5. What other verses mention the listed attributes?

6. What attributes of God are missing from the lesson's list?

7. God's anger is mentioned several times in the Bible. Is this part of vengeance?

8. Why is obedience part of loving God?

9. Why did the demons know God but not love or obey Him?

10. What would you tell a novice Christian to do to fulfill the first commandment?

11. Why are the psalms a way to understand God?

Possess Strong Belief in and Adherence to the Bible as the Authoritative Word of God

> *[16]All Scripture is given by inspiration of God, and is profitable for doctrine, for reproof, for correction, for instruction in righteousness, [17]that the man of God may be complete, thoroughly equipped for every good work (2 Timothy 3:16-17).*

Many people want to live their lives free of religious mandates as they are seeking a personalized spiritual journey. They may value scientific understanding over faith-based understanding. They may want avoid judgment by any religion not fitting into their fast-paced or immoral lifestyle. These reasons align with a personal-centric lifestyle rather than a God-centric one. Perhaps these people believe in God, but not in a way compelling them to discover what God requires of them.

Believing in God is not enough for Jehovah God. Belief in Jehovah God is not supposed to be a tiny spark in a person's life. Real belief becomes the priority for the person who acknowledges Jehovah God is over all parts of their life and who knows the Bible is how He has told us about Himself and what He wants from us.

Many of us are taught from a young age the Bible is the word of God. But have you considered why the Bible is regarded as the instrument of God's communication with humans, or if the Bible is how God speaks to us today? Let's consider some questions together.

- Who wrote the Bible?
- How do we know the Bible hasn't been changed?
- Did God authorize the Bible?
- What about 'the lost books' of the Bible?
- Why does the Bible apply today?
- Is the Bible all that I need?

Who Wrote the Bible?

The Bible consists of 66 books, divided into 39 books in the Old Testament (OT) and 27 books in the New Testament (NT). Over 35 men wrote these books as God inspired them. We are confident of most of the 66 books' authors; some have multiple authors, and a few have an uncertain author. For example, we don't know who wrote Judges or Hebrews, but tradition has assigned them to Samuel and Paul, respectively. Plus, these books' messages harmonize with the teaching of the rest of the Bible and were accepted by our OT fathers and first-century patriarchs.

For the OT, Christians accept the same books accepted by the Jews. The Roman Catholic and Eastern Orthodox Bibles included some books not found in the Jewish Septuagint. First-century Christians accepted our NT books as Scripture and eyewitnesses of Jesus and His teaching or close associates wrote them. The following chart lists the authors of all the Bible books as assigned by clear facts or tradition.

BOOK	AUTHOR
Genesis, Exodus, Leviticus, Numbers, Deuteronomy	Moses
Joshua Judges	Mostly unknown; some of Joshua written by Joshua
Ruth 1 & 2 Samuel 1 & 2 Kings	Ruth - Probably written during Solomon's reign 1&2 Samuel - Jewish tradition is Samuel 1&2 Kings - Jewish tradition is Jeremiah
1 & 2 Chronicles, Ezra	Ezra
Nehemiah	Nehemiah
Esther, Job	Unknown
Psalms	David, Asaph, Sons of Korah, Solomon, Moses, Ethan, Heman, Unknown
Proverbs	Solomon, Agur, Lemuel
Ecclesiastes Song of Solomon	Solomon
Isaiah	Isaiah
Jeremiah, Lamentations	Jeremiah
Ezekiel	Ezekiel
Daniel	Daniel
Hosea	Hosea
Joel	Joel
Amos	Amos
Obadiah	Obadiah
Jonah	Jonah
Micah	Micah
Nahum	Nahum
Habakkuk	Habakkuk
Zephaniah	Zephaniah
Haggai	Haggai
Zechariah	Zechariah
Malachi	Malachi
Matthew	Matthew
Mark	John Mark
Luke	Luke
John	John

Acts	Luke
Romans, 1 & 2 Corinthians, Galatians, Ephesians, Philippians, Colossians, 1 & 2 Thessalonians, 1 & 2 Timothy, Titus, Philemon	Paul
Hebrews	Tradition is Paul
James	James (brother of Jesus)
1 & 2 Peter	Peter
1, 2 & 3 John	John
Jude	Jude
Revelation	John

God inspired these writers to write what He wanted to tell mankind. His written words inform man about Himself, what He wants His followers to do and say, about other faithful believers during good and bad times, how to worship, and so many different things. His words steer man to salvation and eternity.

All Scripture is God-breathed (2 Timothy 3:16a NIV).

A study of the Bible reveals the interwoven nature of the Bible. Over thousands of years, men who did not know each other wrote God's master plan as God guided and inspired them. He "breathed" His words into their heart and out of their pen. God reveals His entire master plan in the gospel message found in the New Testament. The human writers' pens did not write in "God's language" but in the writer's language, using the words and styles of the writer. God meant for man to understand Him, not to be known only to a few.

How Do We Know the Bible Hasn't Been Changed?

Many skeptics claim they cannot trust the Bible because it has copying errors, modified texts, and no originals exist to verify the copies. Internet clickbait screams about translators supporting political interests in their versions.

Indeed, original copies of the Bible are not available for us to compare our original translations. As more manuscripts are copied, the number of potential errors in any document increases. Scribes made original biblical writings on papyrus, skins, parchment, or vellum, which deteriorated over time. This deterioration necessitated the creation of a copy from the original, and continued to require copying as the original copy disintegrated.

- OT variants are extremely uncommon as professional scribes made copies with strictly controlled rules, and copies with errors were destroyed. Found antiquities overwhelmingly confirm the translations we are using now are the same as the ancient texts.

- NT copies did not have the rigorous control that the OT when making copies. For example, Christians distributed Paul's letters worldwide by copying the

> original. Also, when the First-century Christians faced persecution and destruction of their religious documents, many copies were made to be hidden or taken with the Christians as they fled. The copier may have been a professional scribe, but maybe not. The mere number of private copies of the texts increases the chance of errors.

This author discovered that there are 200,000 variations found between today's Bibles and ancient texts! However, this number is less dramatic than it first seems.

- ✓ If a word was spelled differently in any text or manuscript, each instance was considered a variation. Just this one consideration reduces the number of variations to 10,000.
- ✓ 10,000 is still a LARGE number of variations. Most of these variations are due to unintentional mistakes. For example, the original NT text was written in all capital letters with no punctuation or spacing. The copier's eye could skip a line or a set of letters, put some words in twice, or transpose numbers or letters. If the copier wrote as someone spoke or read text, a word could be misunderstood and recorded incorrectly. Additionally, some copiers made intentional changes to a text to adjust it to local grammar. Eliminating these variations takes the errors down to 40 lines or 400 words.

Are these 40 lines a reason to dump the Bible? Centuries ago, a copier or scholar intentionally added these 400 words to clarify or harmonize Biblical teaching. Some ancient manuscripts contain them, and some do not. A close look at these verses shows us the doctrine in them is taught elsewhere in the Bible. These verses are: Mark 16:9-20; John 7:53-8:11; Acts 8:37; and 1 John 5:7.

Early in the second century, the church in Alexandria began comparing copies and standardizing text. In the third century, Emperor Constantine accelerated and managed the careful copying of texts to ensure faithful copies of manuscripts. Still, scholars study artifacts and ancient manuscripts to ensure we have an accurate reproduction of the words God "breathed" so long ago. This excerpt from *From God to Us – How We Got Our Bible* by Norman L Geisler and William E. Nix assures our Bible is the one that God authorized.

> Not only is the Bible the most well-preserved book to survive from the ancient world, its variant readings of significance amount to less than one-half of one percent corruption, none of which affect any basic Christian doctrine. In addition, the textual critic has at his disposal a series of canons which for all practical purposes enables him to completely restore the exact text of the Hebrew and Greek autographs of the Scriptures—not only line for line, but even word for word.

Did God Authorize the Bible?

The inspiration of God caused men to write the Bible. 2 Timothy 3:16-17 are critical verses for this idea. The Scripture is "God-breathed" or "given by inspiration of God," depending on the translation. The Greek word for this phrase is *theopneustos*. It combines the Greek word for God and the Greek word for breath (theos-pneustos).

[16]All Scripture is God-breathed and is useful for teaching, rebuking, correcting and training in righteousness, [17]so that the servant of God may be thoroughly equipped for every good work (2 Timothy 3:16-17 NIV).

The books in our Bibles were written down by men, using their own style of speech and language, controlled by the inspiration of God, as to what they wrote. Either God dictated to them what to write and had already considered the writer's language styles, or He gave them the concepts or thoughts to write down in their language styles. God revealed, and man recorded His words in either of theses methods. The writers had free will, but God inspired them to write and controlled the words.

This process produced the Bible, God's final guidance for His doctrine. Other verses confirm that God speaks to us through the Bible, from ancient times to the present and into the future.

These things we also speak, not in words which man's wisdom teaches but which the Holy Spirit teaches, comparing spiritual things with spiritual (1 Corinthians 2:13).

[20]knowing this first, that no prophecy of Scripture is of any private interpretation, [21]for prophecy never came by the will of man, but holy men of God spoke as they were moved by the Holy Spirit (2 Peter 1:20-21).

What about 'The Lost Books' of the Bible?

An internet search for 'lost books' of the Bible yields an impressive array of titles. This author found a list of 75 lost books through such a search. This website categorizes these lost books as apocryphal or pseudepigraphal texts.

- Apocryphal books have an unknown author or time of writing and do not harmonize with Bible teaching. For example, the Apocalypse of Peter / The Second Apocalypse of James tells the story of Peter's death and descent into hell due to Satan's testing of him.

- Pseudepigraphal books have a false claim of authorship. For example, a book claiming to have been written by Peter, but actually written by someone else, is a pseudepigraphal book. Most of the 75 lost books listed were of this classification. Sometimes, pseudepigraphal books were written centuries after Jesus' life to pursue a specific point of view, such as many Gnostic books.

Often, lost books' teachings were radically different from Jesus' teachings. Some claimed Jesus was merely a human who obtained enlightenment. Others claimed Jesus was a divine creature, not human, and only taught about immortality. Still, others wrote about Jesus' life in a fairytale fashion with mystical overtones. Without known authorship and harmonizing with accepted books of the Bible, these lost books are considered heretical or sinful.

Why Does the Bible Apply Today?

The Bible reveals God's truth to us. God is the same today, yesterday, and tomorrow. So, God is essential to us today, yesterday, and tomorrow. People of the past, people of today, and people of tomorrow all need God. If God is forever, His words in the Bible are true and forever, too.

> *For I am the LORD, I do not change (Malachi 3:6a).*
>
> *The grass withers, the flower fades, But the word of our God stands forever (Isaiah 40:8).*
>
> *Observe and obey all these words which I command you, that it may go well with you and your children after you forever, when you do what is good and right in the sight of the Lord your God (Deuteronomy 12:28).*

Is the Bible All that I Need?

Throughout the centuries, our Bible asserts that the word of God has all the commandments and guidance needed to be righteous before God.

> *Whatever I command you, be careful to observe it; you shall not add to it nor take away from it (Deuteronomy 12:32).*
>
> *You shall not add to the word which I command you, nor take from it, that you may keep the commandments of the Lord your God which I command you (Deuteronomy 4:2).*
>
> *I know that whatever God does, It shall be forever. Nothing can be added to it, And nothing taken from it. God does it, that men should fear before Him (Ecclesiastes 3:14).*

Jesus often contended with the Pharisees, who had made an additional rules to ensure people did not break the Bible's commandments. The Pharisees had considered the Mosaic Law and a compilation of Jewish writings called the Mishnah to develop 613 regulations. These laws had become more important than God's will and were not what the Bible taught.

It is just as important to understand the Bible is our final measure of righteousness. We cannot follow our hearts and do what is right in our own eyes. Instead, we must obey Jesus and find His words and commandments in our Bibles. Remember, Jesus said, "*If any man will come after me, let him deny himself, and take up his cross daily, and follow me*" (Luke 9:23). His commandments always come before our desires—each and every day of our lives.

Summary

The Bible is God's inspired word. It is all we need for teaching and living righteously before God.

Discussion Questions

1. In the introduction, why does the author distinguish between a God and Jehovah God?

2. How did God "breathe" the scriptures?

3. Are copying errors a significant concern to you? Why or why not?

4. Why were NT scribes considered part of the "upper class" by the Jews?

5. Why would commentaries, handbooks, church writings, or other materials not be authorized by God?

6. Under what circumstances would additional "church" materials be beneficial? When would they not be helpful and maybe sinful?

7. Should our Bibles add some of the "lost" books? Why would men from long ago reject them?

8. How do OT writings apply to NT Christians?

9. When would additional rules or commandments like the Pharisees made be beneficial to an NT Christian? Are church by-laws in this classification?

10. Why do you believe the Bible is the word of God?

References

Bynes, S. (2024, March 2). The list of 75 books removed from the Bible. Totally the Dream. https://totallythedream.com/books-removed-from-the-bible/

Geisler, N. L. and Nix, W. E. (1974). From God to Us – How We Got Our Bible. Moody Bible Institute of Chicago. Pages 11-13, 18, 163-164, 176-179, 180-181, 184-186.

Jones, T. P. (2007). *Why Trust the Bible?* Rose Publishing.

The rules of the pharisees. pursueGOD.org. (n.d.). https://www.pursuegod.org/rules-pharisees/

What is the meaning of god-breathed in reference to the Bible?. CompellingTruth.org. (n.d.). https://www.compellingtruth.org/God-breathed.html

Wikipedia Foundation. (2025, July 6). Gnosticism. Wikipedia. https://en.wikipedia.org/wiki/Gnosticism#Jesus_as_Gnostic_saviour

Ability to Consistently Show Love and Compassion toward Others, Including Colleagues and Community Members

And the second is like it: 'You shall love your neighbor as yourself' (Matthew 22:39).

Let's consider this verse in context to understand what Jesus is saying. Jesus contended with Jewish leaders, including the Sadducees, Pharisees, and Herodians, throughout Matthew 21 and 22. Jesus had portrayed the Jewish leaders and Pharisees as wicked in his parables of the two sons and the vinedressers. The chief priests and Pharisees wanted to arrest Jesus but feared the multitudes who believed Jesus was a prophet (Matthew 21:45-46). Jesus continued to portray them as evil in his parable of the wedding feast, so they withdrew to plot and plan against him. Next, the Herodians attempted to trip up Jesus with political arguments about taxes. Jesus answered that it was proper to obey the government unless doing so would be sinful. The next group up to bat was the Sadducees (who only recognized the Pentateuch and did not believe in an afterlife) with questions about a levirate marriage. Jesus sat them down by proving resurrection with verses from the Pentateuch. The last one up to bat is a Pharisee lawyer with a tricky question to rank the Lord's commandments. *"Teacher, which is the great commandment in the law?" (Matthew 22:36).*

37Jesus said to him, "'You shall love the LORD your God with all your heart, with all your soul, and with all your mind.' 38This is the first and great commandment. 39And the second is like it: 'You shall love your neighbor as yourself.' 40On these two commandments hang all the Law and the Prophets" (Matthew 22:37-40).

Love God and your neighbor! The lawyer was trying to create an argument that Jesus could not win. Instead, Jesus summarized the law in two sentences. Look at the Ten Commandments given to Moses to show how these two sentences summarize God's commandments.

Love the Lord with all your heart	Love your neighbor as yourself
No other gods before me	Honor father and mother
No idols	No murder, No adultery,
Not take Lord's name in vain	No stealing, No lying,
Keep Sabbath holy	No coveting

Jesus affirmed this same division for all commandments of the Old Testament in verse 40. However, it is crucial to notice that Jesus' second great commandment is not just what not to do to your neighbor, like the Ten Commandments, but is an action verb of what to do. His commandment is not "don't do bad things to your neighbor." His commandment is to LOVE your neighbor as yourself. We naturally love ourselves and want good things for ourselves. Similarly, God wants us to be concerned for the welfare of others.

Why Does God Care about Our Neighbor?

One of my favorite hymns (*The Greatest Commands* by Kurt Kaiser) answers this question because it uses the words found in 1 John 4:7-8. The verses and the hymn teach that God is love, and we cannot love God if we do not love one another.

> *[7]Beloved, let us love one another, for love is of God; and everyone who loves is born of God and knows God. [8]He who does not love does not know God, for God is love (1 John 4:7-8).*

John is speaking of active goodwill toward our neighbors' welfare, just as Jesus did in His response to the lawyer. We cannot hate our neighbor because they follow another religion, have a barking dog, are a murderer, or look different. One of God's finest attributes is love, and mankind clings to this with our hopes and prayers. This chapter talks about God's love and our love for God and our neighbors. John's warning is firm that we cannot love God, whom we cannot see, and hate our neighbor, whom we can see.

> *[20]If someone says, "I love God," and hates his brother, he is a liar; for he who does not love his brother whom he has seen, how can he love God whom he has not seen? [21]And this commandment we have from Him: that he who loves God must love his brother also (1 John 4:20-21).*

We all know that some people are hard to love. They may be argumentative, scary, disruptive, and very different from us. Here, John is not talking about love in the sense of hearts and roses or family bonds. He is speaking of our active goodwill to all other people. This goodwill extends to our cantankerous neighbor living next door, who never mows their lawn and lets their dog bark all night, to people in prison, to those who look and believe differently than we do, and to people across the globe. God loves all these people and sent His son to save them.

Who is Our Neighbor?

There is a similar story about another lawyer trying to test Jesus in Luke 10:25-37. This lawyer asked about inheriting eternal life. Jesus asked him, "What is written in the law?" The lawyer responded by combining Deuteronomy 6:5 and Leviticus 19:18. Note that every faithful Jew of the day recited Deuteronomy 6:5 twice daily.

> *You shall love the Lord your God with all your heart, with all your soul, and with all your strength (Deuteronomy 6:5).*

> *You shall not take vengeance, nor bear any grudge against the children of your people, but you shall love your neighbor as yourself: I am the Lord (Leviticus 19:18).*

This lawyer wanted more from Jesus' positive response and continued to challenge Jesus. Some commentators think the lawyer was trying to limit his responsibility to neighbors and the demands of the law by having Jesus define boundaries. Others think the lawyer was trying to test Jesus in legal discussions of the law. Either way, Jesus tells us who our neighbor is in the parable of the Good Samaritan.

In the parable, the traveling man was beaten by thieves and left half-dead. A priest and a Levite passed by on the other side of the road to avoid the wounded man. A Samaritan passed by and had compassion for the wounded man. The Samaritan immediately cared for the man on the road and provided for his care as he recovered. At the end of the parable, Jesus asked the lawyer who the neighbor was to the wounded man, and the lawyer responded, "He who showed mercy on him." Jesus told the lawyer, "Go and do likewise."

Jesus told the lawyer to help his neighbor when he had an opportunity, as the Samaritan had done. He is telling us the same!

- The Samaritan put himself at risk from the same thieves who had beaten the traveling man.
- He also used his limited traveling resources to bandage the man and a donkey to get him to a safe place.
- He used his financial resources to provide for the man as he recovered.

The Samaritan used his time and money, taking personal risk, to help someone he did not know, without any assumption of reward in return. This Samaritan loved his neighbor and was a good neighbor. The parable's point is to be a good neighbor to all.

Can Love Be Selective?

The short answer is the only answer to this question—NO! Christian love is not selective and is without partiality. Partiality is sinful, and the gospel condemns it.

> *8 If you really fulfill the royal law according to the Scripture, "You shall love your neighbor as yourself," you do well; 9 but if you show partiality, you commit sin, and are convicted by the law as transgressors (James 2:8-9).*

The preceding verses of James 2 warn us against partiality with the example of a rich man and a poor man coming into the assembly. A Christian cannot prefer a person with gold rings and fine clothes to a man in dirty clothes. James reminded the first-century Christians that God had chosen the poor to be rich in faith. Both the rich man and the poor man are our neighbors. However, a Christian cannot prefer to love the rich man over the poor man. A rich man can return our favor, while a poor man probably cannot.

Why Is Love for Others Important?

Christians fulfill the law of Christ with love. Our God is love, so we must love with active goodwill toward all people.

> *For all the law is fulfilled in one word, even in this: "You shall love your neighbor as yourself" (Galatians 5:14).*

> *If you really fulfill the royal law according to the Scripture, "You shall love your neighbor as yourself," you do well (James 2:8).*

Christians demonstrate God's love with loving actions toward others. The wonderful thing about our demonstrations is that they are not required to be big, but we are required to look for opportunities. Our neighbors can be sick, depressed, stressed, or tired. They can be familiar to us or strangers whom we meet. They can live beside us, in the same city, state, or any where in the world. In today's world, neighbors can be just about anybody and live anywhere.

However, these verses do not teach that we are responsible for helping every person in the world. We are responsible for helping those we can help with love.

- We might help someone living with famine in Africa with a few dollars. We cannot solve the famine or feed everyone on the continent, but we can help someone.
- We might provide a meal to a sick coworker. We don't have to prepare every meal, but we do what we can.
- We might support a preacher in another country with a care package. We cannot provide him with total support, but we can encourage him.
- We might provide a used table to someone whose house has burned. From time to time, some of us have extra furniture another person can use.
- We might babysit for a stressed mother. Babysitting costs us only time, but provides invaluable relief to a mother.
- We might send cards to sick friends. A card tells the receiver they are remembered, which is especially important to those with long-term conditions.
- We might visit or call the elderly in assisted living or a nursing home. Even a short visit can be the highlight of this person's day. Remember, God loves sick people, also.
- We might use our skills to provide a service to someone needing encouragement. All of us have different skills. We must look for a way to use them to serve others.

No list can identify how a Christian can love a neighbor or all the people a neighbor might be. Each of us will have different opportunities to love and help a neighbor. It is our responsibility to recognize the opportunities and find a ways to act on them. Christian love is not a lazy lifestyle but a busy one.

Why this Commandment?

We must love because God loves. Genesis 1 explains so well the reason God loves. After every day of creation, God looked at what he had done and saw it was good. On the sixth day, man was made in God's own image, both male and female. "Then God blessed them, and God said to them, 'Be fruitful and multiply; fill the earth and subdue it; have dominion over the fish of the sea, over the birds of the air, and over every living thing that moves on the earth'" (Genesis 1:28). The last verse of the chapter affirms that God's creation was good.

> *Then God saw everything that He had made, and indeed it was very good. So the evening and the morning were the sixth day (Genesis 1:31).*

God has continued to love and care for mankind throughout time. The strongest evidence of this love is how God provided the pathway to eternal life with Him.

[16]For God so loved the world that He gave His only begotten Son, that whoever believes in Him should not perish but have everlasting life. [17]For God did not send His Son into the world to condemn the world, but that the world through Him might be saved (John 3:16-17).

And she will bring forth a Son, and you shall call His name Jesus, for He will save His people from their sins" (Matthew 1:21).

God loves mankind—all of them and has since He created man and woman in Genesis 1. If God can care for the righteous and the sinful, why shouldn't He want us to follow His example? God's plan includes active goodwill among all the people that He has made. He has commanded us to love one another because He loves us all.

Summary

God wants His people to love their neighbors and has repeatedly commanded His people to love. A verse from Romans summarizes this lesson very well.

[8]Owe no one anything except to love one another, for he who loves another has fulfilled the law. [9]For the commandments, "You shall not commit adultery," "You shall not murder," "You shall not steal," "You shall not bear false witness," "You shall not covet," and if there is any other commandment, are all summed up in this saying, namely, "You shall love your neighbor as yourself." [10]Love does no harm to a neighbor; therefore love is the fulfillment of the law (Romans 13:8-10).

Discussion Questions

1. How is Leviticus 19:18 similar to the second great commandment in Matthew 22:37? How are they different?

2. How is love for our neighbor different than our love for family and friends?

3. If God is love, how does that affect a Christian's love for a neighbor?

4. In Luke 10:25-37, why did the lawyer challenge Jesus about neighbors?

5. Do all of us have the same opportunities to love our neighbors?

6. Does the commandment to love our neighbor require a response to every request made to us?

7. How would you explain to a new Christian how to love their neighbor?

8. Why is partiality a danger to fulfilling the commandment to love your neighbor?

9. Why has God commanded us to love our neighbor?

Willingness to Undergo and Affirm the Act of Baptism

Have you ever noticed that first-century Christians never asked what baptism was in the New Testament? No one asked because the idea of ritualized washing was familiar to them. We don't have as much ritualized washing as was common during the first-century, so we aren't always sure what it is. Today, baptism is often defined as an outward sign of an inward conversion or inward grace, but is it?

Wikipedia tells us a lot about the etyomology of the word "baptism." The following is quoted directly from their website, so the ancient words are presented accurately.

> The English word baptism is derived indirectly through Latin from the neuter Greek concept noun báptisma (Greek βάπτισμα, "washing, dipping"),which is a neologism in the New Testament derived from the masculine Greek noun baptismós (βαπτισμός), a term for ritual washing in Greek language texts of Hellenistic Judaism during the Second Temple period, such as the Septuagint. Both of these nouns are derived from the verb baptízō (βαπτίζω, "I wash" transitive verb), which is used in Jewish texts for ritual washing, and in the New Testament both for ritual washing and also for the apparently new rite of báptisma.
>
> The Greek verb báptō (βάπτω), "dip", from which the verb baptízō is derived, is in turn hypothetically traced to a reconstructed Indo-European root *g^{w}abh-, "dip".
>
> The Greek words are used in a great variety of meanings. βάπτω and βαπτίζω in Hellenism had the general usage of "immersion," "going under" (as a material in a liquid dye) or "perishing" (as in a ship sinking or a person drowning), with the same double meanings as in English "to sink into" or "to be overwhelmed by," with bathing or washing only occasionally used and usually in sacral contexts.

Old Testament Practices

The old law commanded ritualized washings for men, women, and priests. The following are a few washing commandments found in Leviticus.

1. *Leviticus 14 (skin diseases) - [8]He who is to be cleansed shall wash his clothes, shave off all his hair, and wash himself in water, that he may be clean. After that he shall come into the camp, and shall stay outside his tent seven days. [9]But on the seventh day he shall shave all the hair off his head and his beard and his eyebrows—all his hair he shall shave off. He shall wash his clothes and wash his body in water, and he shall be clean (Lev. 14:8-9).*
2. *Leviticus 15 (bodily fluids) - And when he who has a discharge is cleansed of his discharge, then he shall count for himself seven days for his cleansing, wash his clothes, and bathe his body in running water; then he shall be clean (Lev. 15:13).*

(women's monthly cycles) - [21]Whoever touches her bed shall wash his clothes and bathe in water, and be unclean until evening. [22]And whoever touches anything that she sat on shall wash his clothes and bathe in water, and be unclean until evening (Lev. 15:21-22).

3. *Leviticus 16 (Aaron before entering Most Holy Place) - [4]He shall put the holy linen tunic and the linen trousers on his body; he shall be girded with a linen sash, and with the linen turban he shall be attired. These are holy garments. Therefore he shall wash his body in water, and put them on (Lev. 16:4).*
   (the person who released the scapegoat before reentering camp) - And he who released the goat as the scapegoat shall wash his clothes and bathe his body in water, and afterward he may come into the camp (Lev. 16:26).
4. *Leviticus 17 (eating unclean meat) - "And every person who eats what died naturally or what was torn by beasts, whether he is a native of your own country or a stranger, he shall both wash his clothes and bathe in water, and be unclean until evening. Then he shall be clean (Lev. 17:15).*

It is important to note that this is a partial list! For an idea of the importance of purity, the word or derivatives "wash" are in Leviticus, Numbers, and Deuteronomy 47 times, "clean" 80 times, and "bathe" 18 times.

Old Testament Cleansings

We read about ritual cleansings throughout the OT. In Exodus 19:10-11, God gave the Israelites three days to cleanse themselves. Leviticus 16 commanded Levite priests to cleanse themselves in water before and after their priestly duties (Lev. 16:4; 16:23-24). We must remember that Elisha commanded Naaman to wash in the Jordan River to be cured of his leprosy (2 Kings 5)! Shadows of baptism to wash for purity are throughout the OT.

Rabbinic standards developed during the Second Temple period (516 BCE–70 CE) defined the amount water required for these ritual cleansings and how the person was to use the water. A mikveh containing about 150 gallons of water (enough to cover an average-sized man) was required. The mikveh had to be connected to naturally occurring waters, like a spring or rainwater. A person performed the ritual cleansing by immersing their body into the mikveh, ensuring that the water touched every part of their body.. Mikvehs and other washing pools were common in the first century.

Enough water to cover an average-sized man's body must also have been John the Baptist's requirement. He required "*much water*" when baptizing in Aenon near Salim (John 3:23). In Acts 8, the Ethiopian eunuch could see some water while driving with Philip in his chariot. After noticing this water, the eunuch asked to be baptized.

John's Baptism

John the Baptist, Jesus' cousin, performed the first baptisms mentioned in the NT. John preached about the coming of Christ to *prepare the way of the Lord and make His paths straight*, just as messengers were sent ahead to prepare the way for earthly kings and the places being visited and to smooth the roads before the king's visit.

[4]John came baptizing in the wilderness and preaching a baptism of repentance for the remission of sins. [5]Then all the land of Judea, and those from Jerusalem, went out to him and were all baptized by him in the Jordan River, confessing their sins (Mark 1:4-5).

However, John's baptism is not the same as Jesus' baptism. John's baptism was to prepare his hearers for the King. The preposition "for" in verse 4 could also be translated as "with a view to." John was preparing his audience for repentance, leading to God's forgiveness of sins in Jesus' baptism. His baptism was a preparation, not a final act. Apollos demonstrated this in Acts 18. Apollos had been baptized with John's baptism, but Priscilla and Aquila taught him that gospel baptism was required for the remission of sins.

[24]Now a certain Jew named Apollos, born at Alexandria, an eloquent man and mighty in the Scriptures, came to Ephesus. [25]This man had been instructed in the way of the Lord; and being fervent in spirit, he spoke and taught accurately the things of the Lord, though he knew only the baptism of John. [26]So he began to speak boldly in the synagogue. When Aquila and Priscilla heard him, they took him aside and explained to him the way of God more accurately (Acts 18:24-26).

Jesus' baptism symbolizes our spiritual death, burial, and resurrection with Christ. It is preceded by hearing and believing the gospel, repenting of sins, and confessing our faith in the name of Jesus Christ. The baptism of the gospel is not to prepare us for the coming of the King, but to proclaim the King is here and we are His children.

What Is Commanded in NT for Us?

The NT commands baptism after people believe in Jesus Christ and repent of their sins. The best examples are in Acts, but Acts 2:38 speaks very clearly. In Acts 2, Peter commands them, "Repent, and let every one of you be baptized in the name of Jesus Christ for the remission of sins; and you shall receive the gift of the Holy Spirit" (Acts 2:38).

Belief in Jesus Christ is the essential first step, and repentance for sins closely follows. When the people on Pentecost believed in Jesus, they were cut to the heart and asked Peter what they should do (Acts 2:37). Peter tells them, "Repent, and let every one of you be baptized in the name of Jesus Christ for the remission of sins." Verse 41 tells us that three thousand souls were added to the church that day.

Jesus gave us the 'Great Commission' in three gospels. We are to teach others so they can believe, repent, and then be baptized to be saved.

[19]Go therefore and make disciples of all the nations, baptizing them in the name of the Father and of the Son and of the Holy Spirit, [20]teaching them to observe all things that I have commanded you; and lo, I am with you always, even to the end of the age." Amen (Matthew 28:19-20).

[15]And He said to them, "Go into all the world and preach the gospel to every creature. [16]He who believes and is baptized will be saved; but he who does not believe will be condemned (Mark 16:15-16).

And that repentance and remission of sins should be preached in His name to all nations, beginning at Jerusalem (Luke 24:47).

Why Must We Be Cleansed?

God is holy and righteous. He hates sin, and all of us are sinners. We must be baptized to be cleansed from sin and made righteous before God. The water of baptism is the answer of a good conscience toward God (1 Peter 3:21b).

> [20]*Who formerly were disobedient, when once the Divine longsuffering waited in the days of Noah, while the ark was being prepared, in which a few, that is, eight souls, were saved through water.* [21]*There is also an antitype which now saves us—baptism (not the removal of the filth of the flesh, but the answer of a good conscience toward God), through the resurrection of Jesus Christ (1 Pet. 3:20-21).*

Hebrews 10:22 affirms we must be washed to draw near to God. God is faithful to those who seek Him, but He has conditions for those who are allowed close to Him. They must have an honest and open heart, have obedient and loving faith in Jesus Christ, and have the blood of Jesus' sacrifice sprinkled on their heart to cleanse their conscience and wash their bodies in pure water for their sins.

> *Let us draw near with a true heart in full assurance of faith, having our hearts sprinkled from an evil conscience and our bodies washed with pure water (Hebrews 10:22).*

We cannot be with God while we are sinners. Baptism takes away our sins. On the road to Damascus, Jesus had told Paul, "*And now why are you waiting? Arise and be baptized, and wash away your sins, calling on the name of the Lord*" (Acts 22:16). Baptism took away Paul's sins, and he had plenty of them! It will also wash away our sins.

Who Does God Want to Save?

Salvation is for everyone. God loves all His creation and wants all His people to be saved and live with Him forever. However, individuals who do not choose to believe and obey will not receive everlasting life.

> [16]*For God so loved the world that He gave His only begotten Son, that whoever believes in Him should not perish but have everlasting life.* [17]*For God did not send His Son into the world to condemn the world, but that the world through Him might be saved.* [18]*"He who believes in Him is not condemned; but he who does not believe is condemned already, because he has not believed in the name of the only begotten Son of God (John 3:16-18).*

Persons who are ready to be baptized are those who have been taught, have believed in Jesus, have repented of their sins, and have confessed their faith. The following verses confirm these ideas and apply to us today.

- *teaching them to observe all things that I have commanded you (Matthew 28:20a)*
- *He who believes and is baptized will be saved (Mark 16:16a)*

- *Repent, and let every one of you be baptized in the name of Jesus Christ for the remission of sins (Acts 2:38a)*
- *[36b]And the eunuch said, "See, here is water. What hinders me from being baptized?" [37]Then Philip said, "If you believe with all your heart, you may." And he answered and said, "I believe that Jesus Christ is the Son of God" (Acts 8:36b-37)*

When Are We Baptized?

The story of the Philippian jailer found in Acts 16:25-34 is an excellent example of the immediate need for baptism after belief and repentance. The jailer asked Paul and Silas what he must do to be saved, and they replied to believe in Jesus and preached to the jailer. The jailer believed and demonstrated repentance by washing the wounds of Paul and Silas. The jailer's understanding of the word of the Lord required immediate baptism. Paul and Silas taught him that baptism was necessary for salvation, or why did he know to be baptized? He did not wait for daylight or for public baths to open. He wanted salvation, believed in the Lord Jesus Christ, and knew from the preaching of Paul and Silas that baptism was necessary. He was baptized that night, not at a convenient time.

Similarly, the Ethiopian eunuch, after being taught by Philip, said, "*See, here is water. What hinders me from being baptized*" (Acts 8:36b). The eunuch did not wait to be baptized after understanding its requirement.

After the Romans arrested Paul in Jerusalem, he gave a sermon to the Jews while standing on the steps of the Roman garrison attached to the northwest side of the temple. Paul said Ananias had told him, "*And now why are you waiting? Arise and be baptized, and wash away your sins, calling on the name of the Lord*" (Acts 22:16).

The Philippian jailer, the Ethiopian eunuch, and Paul were immediately baptized after understanding the requirement.

What About Grace?

> *[8] For by grace you have been saved through faith, and that not of yourselves; it is the gift of God, [9] not of works, lest anyone should boast (Ephesians 2:8-9).*
>
> *There is also an antitype which now saves us—baptism (not the removal of the filth of the flesh, but the answer of a good conscience toward God), through the resurrection of Jesus Christ (1 Peter 3:21).*

If grace saves us through our faith, why does one need to be baptized? How is 1 Peter 3:21 reconciled with Ephesians 2:8-9?

First, I hope we can agree that we need God's grace to be saved. None of us can keep God's commandments perfectly. We require His unmerited favor to be saved as we cannot work or earn our way into heaven. However, baptism is God's plan for us to be baptized into Jesus' death (Romans 6:3), not to wash our bodies. Baptism employs our faith to fulfill God's commandment for baptism and is not a personal work.

Baptism and grace are both necessary for our salvation. The Bible tells us so.

Summary

Baptism is not an outward sign of an inward conversion or grace, but is a commandment from God. Salvation requires baptism for all who believe in Jesus, repent their sins, and confess of their faith. Baptism is water immersion and saves us from our sins. Believers are baptized with joy and gladness soon after they realize God has commanded it.

Discussion Questions

1. Why does the etyomology of the word 'baptism' matter to a Christian?

2. How do OT commandments for ritualized washing shadow today's commandment for baptism?

3. How does the ancient Jewish use of a mikveh affect today's baptism?

4. How would you explain the difference between John's baptism and Jesus' baptism?

5. What verse(s) would you use to show someone that baptism is required?

6. How can water cleanse us from sin and make us righteous before God?

7. If God sent His Son to save the world, why does the author claim only those who have been taught, believed, repented, and confessed can be baptized?

8. Why is immediate baptism necessary? Or is it?

9. How do baptism and grace work together?

References

https://westpalmbeachchurchofchrist.com/topical/rethinking_scriptures/baptism-and-old-testament.html
https://en.wikipedia.org/wiki/Baptism
https://www.gotquestions.org/origin-baptism.html
https://www.compellingtruth.org/baptism-Old-Testament.html

Active Participation in Regular Public Worship Services and Gatherings

The Covid pandemic, social media, and our personal preferences often cause us to limit our face-to-face interactions with others. However, gathering together to worship God and fellowship with others is a commandments from God. Even in the Old Testament (OT), God's people formally assembled. Exodus 12 has several commanded assemblies and the Passover feast. For example, [16]*On the first day there shall be a holy convocation, and on the seventh day there shall be a holy convocation for you. No manner of work shall be done on them; but that which everyone must eat—that only may be prepared by you* (Exodus 12:16). Assembling for worship on the Sabbath was commanded for the OT Jews. *Likewise the people of the land shall worship at the entrance to this gateway before the Lord on the Sabbaths and the New Moons* (Ezekiel 46:3).

Similarly, the New Testament (NT) commands Christians to gather together for worship. We can learn how God wants this worship to proceed by reviewing NT commands and examples.

When to Worship Publically

The OT commanded the Jews to worship on the Sabbath, the last day of the week. God set an example for them when He rested on the seventh day of creation (Genesis 2:2). The best-known verses with this commandment are found in Exodus 20 and are part of the Ten Commandments. [8] *"Remember the Sabbath day, to keep it holy.* [9] *Six days you shall labor and do all your work,* [10] *but the seventh day is the Sabbath of the Lord your God. In it you shall do no work: you, nor your son, nor your daughter, nor your male servant, nor your female servant, nor your cattle, nor your stranger who is within your gates.* [11] *For in six days the Lord made the heavens and the earth, the sea, and all that is in them, and rested the seventh day. Therefore the Lord blessed the Sabbath day and hallowed it* (Exodus 20:8-11).

Similarly, Christians are to worship on the first day of the week, as this is the day Jesus arose from the dead, and we have examples of first-century Christians worshipping on this day. [1]*Now on the first day of the week, very early in the morning, they, and certain other women with them, came to the tomb bringing the spices which they had prepared.* [2]*But they found the stone rolled away from the tomb* (Luke 24:1-2).

Acts 20 contains the best New Testament verse of first-century Christians coming together for worship on the first day of the week. *Now on the first day of the week, when the disciples came together to break bread, Paul, ready to depart the next day, spoke to them and continued his message until midnight* (Acts 20:7). In this one verse are examples of a first day of the week assembly, the breaking of bread, and a sermon! This breaking of bread involved sharing bread and wine to remember Jesus' death and resurrection, often called the Lord's Supper.

Christians may assemble at other times for Bible study, fellowship, or other reasons, not just on Sunday. These assemblies may be authorized by church elders or initiated by individual Christians. Good examples of this are mid-week Bible studies or periodic singings for all congregation members. Individual Christians can hold Bible studies or start specific projects to help a church group or certain people. There is never a wrong time to assemble or study with other Christians in God's kingdom, but the commanded public worship is on Sunday.

First-Day-of-the-Week Worship

IN SPIRIT AND TRUTH

Jesus told the Samaritan woman, *"[23]But the hour is coming, and now is, when the true worshipers will worship the Father in spirit and truth; for the Father is seeking such to worship Him. [24]God is Spirit, and those who worship Him must worship in spirit and truth"* (John 4:23-24). Worshipping in spirit involves the Christian's whole heart. We cannot just show up for an hour to warm a pew while we think about lunch. Full engagement of our attitudes and thoughts is required to worship in spirit. God is Spirit, and our spirits must worship Him! Worshipping in truth ensures the gospel is the gold standard to align us with the will of God. This type of worship is not a passive activity for us to endure, but a total commitment complete with involvement, attentiveness, mindfulness, and introspection.

In his first letter to the Corinthians, Paul admonished them to be more organized when they came together. Commotions with simultaneous speakers, non-understandable languages, and other disruptive activities were not conducive to worship or teaching of the gospel. Individual worship services are not organized exactly the same, but all the components should be in the plan.

> *Let all things be done decently and in order (1 Corinthians 14:40).*

The New Testament shows us that our first-day-of-the-week commanded worship consists of five activities: the Lord's Supper, singing, prayer, teaching/preaching, and giving.

LORD'S SUPPER

The purpose of the Lord's Supper is to remember Jesus' sacrifice, His death and resurrection, which began the new covenant that Christians have with God. His victory over death ended the covenant with all the laws and sacrifices described in the Old Testament. As we share the Lord's Supper with others, we remember Jesus offered Himself as the last and perfect sacrifice to confirm this new covenant, which lasts until Jesus comes again.

> *[23]For I received from the Lord that which I also delivered to you: that the Lord Jesus on the same night in which He was betrayed took bread; [24]and when He had given thanks, He broke it and said,]"Take, eat; this is My body which is*

broken for you; do this in remembrance of Me." [25] *In the same manner He also took the cup after supper, saying, "This cup is the new covenant in My blood. This do, as often as you drink it, in remembrance of Me."* [26] *For as often as you eat this bread and drink this cup, you proclaim the Lord's death till He comes (1 Corinthians 11:23-26).*

Jesus was born to save us from our sins (Matthew 1:21) and was the spotless lamb, the perfect sacrifice for our redemption. His death ended the endless cycle of blood from animals required for OT sacrifices. No other sacrifice is necessary, as Jesus was the final one. We share the Lord's Supper with one another each Sunday to remember His suffering and sacrifice for us.

[11] *And every priest stands ministering daily and offering repeatedly the same sacrifices, which can never take away sins.* [12] *But this Man, after He had offered one sacrifice for sins forever, sat down at the right hand of God,* [13] *from that time waiting till His enemies are made His footstool.* [14] *For by one offering He has perfected forever those who are being sanctified (Hebrews 10:11-14).*

As we partake of the Lord's Supper and remember Jesus' sacrifice on the cross, we must judge ourselves and inventory our strengths, weaknesses, and actions for constant improvement. This personal examination ensures we partake of the Lord's Supper worthily so that God will not condemn us.

[27] *Therefore whoever eats this bread or drinks this cup of the Lord in an unworthy manner will be guilty of the body and blood of the Lord.* [28] *But let a man examine himself, and so let him eat of the bread and drink of the cup.* [29] *For he who eats and drinks in an unworthy manner eats and drinks judgment to himself, not discerning the Lord's body.* [30] *For this reason many are weak and sick among you, and many sleep.* [31] *For if we would judge ourselves, we would not be judged.* [32] *But when we are judged, we are chastened by the Lord, that we may not be condemned with the world (1 Corinthians 11:27-32).*

SINGING

Plato once said, "Music gives a soul to the universe, wings to the mind, flight to the imagination and life to everything." However, the purpose of music in a worship service differs from Plato's thoughts about music.

1. It praises our omnipresent, omnipotent, and omniscient God, our great and glorious I AM.
2. It informs those who are singing and those who are listening about God.

Let the word of Christ dwell in you richly in all wisdom, teaching and admonishing one another in psalms and hymns and spiritual songs, singing with grace in your hearts to the Lord (Colossians 3:16).

[19] *speaking to one another in psalms and hymns and spiritual songs, singing and making melody in your heart to the Lord,* [20] *giving thanks always for all things to God the Father in the name of our Lord Jesus Christ (Ephesians 5:19-20).*

The critical verbs in the above verses are singing, speaking, teaching, and admonishing. All are action verbs and require activity and effort for the worshipper. Making melody in your heart is not listening and enjoying the singing, but sincerely singing to the Lord with your whole heart. The purpose of music in worship is not to entertain the listener like a spectator sport but to praise God and teach each other. Of course, Christians should also enjoy the music they sing, as there will be lots of singing in heaven!

These verses also indicate vocal music, not instrumental. Singing is with a person's mouth and vocal cords. The New Testament does not command instruments, nor is there an example of instruments in worship in the NT. The Old Testament has examples of instruments in worship. However, Jesus gave us a new covenant with new commandments, examples, and requirements. If a person decides to keep the old law, they must keep all of it. David used instruments (2 Samuel 6:15), but also sacrificed oxen and fatlings (2 Samuel 6:13), danced before God wearing only an ephod (2 Samuel 6:14), and had more than one wife (1 Samuel 25:43).

> *For whoever shall keep the whole law, and yet stumble in one point, he is guilty of all (James 2:10).*

PRAYING

Prayer is an address or petition to God which may be spoken or thought. Prayer in formal worship involves one person saying a prayer while other worshippers listen and/or think of their own prayer. Often, the speaker of a public prayer uses more formal language, but this is not a requirement. We should always respect God as He is God, but big words and flowery language are unnecessary in public or private prayers.

> *[16]Rejoice always, [17]pray without ceasing, [18]in everything give thanks; for this is the will of God in Christ Jesus for you (1 Thessalonians 5:16-18).*

> *[6]Be anxious for nothing, but in everything by prayer and supplication, with thanksgiving, let your requests be made known to God; [7] and the peace of God, which surpasses all understanding, will guard your hearts and minds through Christ Jesus (Philippians 4:6-7).*

Prayers have several parts. However, all the parts may not be included in each prayer. These parts are our adoration of God, confessions of faith, wrongdoing, and repentance, requests for ourselves and others, thankfulness to God, and praises to God.

TEACHING/PREACHING

Acts 20:7 (quoted above) tells us that Paul preached with the Christians at Troas on the first day of the week. In this example, Paul preached until daybreak before he sailed for Assos. The author does not attest that a long sermon is required for formal worship or that all of Paul's sermons were long, but we may occasionally have the opportunity to listen to lengthy lessons.

Listening to gospel-based lessons as part of formal worship is how each Christian grows in the Spirit of God and increases their knowledge of the gospel. Also, sermons are tools to introduce others to the gospel. These formal lessons have many applications for anyone who will listen and learn. Many people will never believe the gospel if they never hear it preached.

> *How then shall they call on Him in whom they have not believed? And how shall they believe in Him of whom they have not heard? And how shall they hear without a preacher? (Romans 10:14).*

Preaching the gospel is part of formal worship but is not limited to Sundays. Daily, Jesus' disciples preached as they went about their lives. The following are two examples.

> *So when they had testified and preached the word of the Lord, they returned to Jerusalem, preaching the gospel in many villages of the Samaritans (Acts 8:25).*

> *And when they had preached the gospel to that city and made many disciples, they returned to Lystra, Iconium, and Antioch (Acts 14:21).*

GIVING

1 Corinthians 16:2 commands giving on the first day of the week. *On the first day of the week let each one of you lay something aside, storing up as he may prosper, that there be no collections when I come* (1 Corinthians 16:2)

This giving is not a tithe as commanded in the Old Law. The Old Testament formally stated the tithing amount. For example, *And concerning the tithe of the herd or the flock, of whatever passes under the rod, the tenth one shall be holy to the Lord* (Leviticus 27:32).

Under the gospel's new covenant, the amount given is freely determined by the giver (as he may prosper) and put in a common treasury (*no collections when I come*). No gospel commandment determines the specific amount, nor is the amount reviewed by any church official. This giving is totally between the giver and God. The giver's attitude is more important to God. We are taught to give 'not grudgingly or by necessity,' but with prayerful forethought and deliberation. Our attitude matters!

> *So let each one give as he purposes in his heart, not grudgingly or of necessity; for God loves a cheerful giver* (2 Corinthians 9:7).

> *He who exhorts, in exhortation; he who gives, with liberality; he who leads, with diligence; he who shows mercy, with cheerfulness* (Romans 12:8).

Giving as part of worship supports the church's work and is necessary for each Christian. However, this 'formal' giving is not the only giving for Christians. Christians will always have opportunities to give to others. We give our time, possessions, or money because we remember that whatever we have already belongs to God, and we are just the stewards of it.

Therefore, as we have opportunity, let us do good to all, especially to those who are of the household of faith (Galatians 6:10).

Fellowship

Assemblies to worship God also have a secondary benefit. Time with other Christians to fellowship! Fellowship is a friendly relationship among people with similar interests. Christians are spiritual brothers and sisters, a family, and the adopted children of God. The first-century Christians spent a lot of time with each other to build earthly bonds within their new family. Familial fellowship is more than a work or club relationship. Christian fellowship is shared joy and pain throughout our earthly lives, because God is our Father and we are His family.

And they continued steadfastly in the apostles' doctrine and fellowship, in the breaking of bread, and in prayers (Acts 2:42).

The Hebrew writer encouraged Jewish Christians to keep strong bonds with each other, to stir up love and good works. First-century Christians needed the fellowship of other Christians and we do too!

[24]*And let us consider one another in order to stir up love and good works,* [25]*not forsaking the assembling of ourselves together, as is the manner of some, but exhorting one another, and so much the more as you see the Day approaching* (Hebrews 10:24-25).

Tradition

Most church groups have traditions, such as standing for an invitation song. Neither the invitation song nor the standing while singing this song is mentioned in the New Testament. It is a tradition to encourage people to accept the gospel message at the end of a church service. However, Christians must ensure traditions are not taught as gospel doctrine. Singing an invitation song is man's tradition, not a commandment from God. It is not sinful to eliminate an invitation song, but it is sinful never to encourage someone to obey the gospel. We must ensure we worship God as He wants us to worship Him.

[6] *He answered and said to them, "Well did Isaiah prophesy of you hypocrites, as it is written: 'This people honors Me with their lips, But their heart is far from Me.* [7] *And in vain they worship Me, Teaching as doctrines the commandments of men.'* [8] *For laying aside the commandment of God, you hold the tradition of men—the washing of pitchers and cups, and many other such things you do"* (Mark 7:6-8).

Summary

Assembling with other Christians to worship God on Sunday is a commandment in the new covenant. This worship consists of remembering Christ's death and resurrection with the Lord's Supper, singing, praying, teaching, and giving. We must worship God in spirit and truth, in an orderly manner, and as He wants.

Discussion Questions

1. What is the difference between a worship service and a Wednesday night service?

2. How can Christians assemble on the first day of the week if they or their family are sick, homebound, working, traveling or have social anxieties?

3. How can we ensure that we are worshipping in spirit and truth?

4. How can differences in opinion about an orderly service be resolved?

5. How do we 'examine' ourselves to be worthy of the Lord's Supper?

6. During worship, is it sinful not to sing if you have a cough, sore throat, or other impediment? What if you have no singing talent?

7. How is instrumental music included in worship?

8. How many prayers are necessary for a worship service?

9. Does Eutychus' example show we can go to sleep during preaching?

10. What should we know about another person's giving on the first day of the week? About their giving on any other day?

11. What does 2 Corinthians 8:1-4 teach us about giving?

12. What traditions are in your worship service? Are they taught as doctrine (God's commandment)?

13. How can we fellowship today?

Job Requirement # 6

Commitment to Maintaining a Personal Devotional Life, Including Prayer and Reflection

The Covid pandemic, social media, and our personal preferences often cause us to limit our interactions with friends and family, and we don't want to share personal aspects of our lives with them either. However, we should never limit our time with God. God has wanted an intimate relationship with His people since He walked in the garden with Adam and Eve. He still wants that relationship with us today. We have our private time with God whenever we pray and meditate on things about God. Prayer is our active communication with God; meditation is when we think about God and His word.

Webster's dictionary defines prayer as "an address (such as a petition) to God or a god in word or thought" and meditation as "a discourse intended to express its author's reflections or to guide others in contemplation." For discourse, Webster's gives "conversatio'" as a synonym and "orderly thought" as an archaic meaning. What does God's word teach us about prayer and meditation?

What Is Prayer?

The word pray(er) first occurs in Genesis 20 when Abraham allowed Abimelech, king of Gerar, to believe Sarah was not already married and to take Sarah for his wife to initiate a political alliance with Abraham. God came to Abimelech in a dream, telling him to give Sarah back to Abraham, for Abraham was a prophet, and then Abraham would pray for Abimelech.

Further perusals of the word's occurrences show an active communication with man and God. Some examples are Samson's prayer for strength (Judges 16:28), Hannah's prayers for a child (1 Samuel 1:10, 12), Samuel's prayers when Israel asked for a king (1 Samuel 8:6), Solomon's public prayer for the new temple (1 Kings 8:22-53), the disciples' prayers to select Judas' replacement (Acts 1:24), and Peter before healing Tabitha (Acts 9:40). All these examples show private and public prayers from individuals speaking directly to God with praise and their concerns or requests.

Jesus' disciples observed Him frequently praying. In Luke 11, they asked Jesus to teach them to pray. His reply, in verses 2-13, teaches us a lot about prayer.

- Verses 2-4 show us that our words are spoken directly to God with praise, respect, and our requests and concerns. Our prayers to God should have a familiar feel, like a conversation with the family member who is our Father in heaven.
- Verses 5-10 teach that we approach God with boldness and persistence. Repeated requests in our prayers for our needs (real and perceived) are pleasing to God.
- Verses 11-13 explain that our heavenly Father will give us more than earthly fathers ever can. His gift of the Holy Spirit surpasses all our earthly needs and requests.

Consider Jesus' prayer on Gethsemane (Matthew 26:38-44). Knowing that God was listening, He spoke directly to God with His worries and fears. His appeal for relief from the necessity of the cross was clear and repeated. And finally, Jesus accepted God's command.

Prayers can be short or long but are generally specific. In that moment, Samson asked for strength to bring one more blow to the Philistines with one sentence. Hannah prayed a long time for a child (long enough for Eli to believe she was drunk). John 17:1-26 records Jesus' longest recorded prayer. This intimate prayer between Jesus and God has specific requests from Jesus. He prays for Himself, His disciples, and all believers. Our prayers can be short 'arrow' prayers or more extended conversations with God. God knows our situations just as a father knows his son needs food. However, He wants us to have a friendly and familiar relationship with Him, so that we tell Him of our requests and concerns in prayer.

What Is in a Prayer?

We studied in Lesson 5 that prayer can consist of our adoration of God, confessions of faith, wrongdoing, and repentance, requests for ourselves and others, and thankfulness and praises to God. Note that each prayer does not require all these mentioned features, but our prayers with God over time do require them.

Adoration of God: The last two verses of Jude are an excellent example of adoration to God. The verses acknowledge the glory of God and our dependence on Him.

> *24Now to Him who is able to keep you from stumbling, And to present you faultless Before the presence of His glory with exceeding joy, 25To God our Savior, Who alone is wise, Be glory and majesty, Dominion and power, Both now and forever. Amen (Jude 24-25).*

Confessions of faith, wrongdoing, and repentance: The first examples of prayers that come to mind for this author involving confessions of faith, wrongdoing, and repentance are those of David. David's relationship with God was strong, but David was a man who sometimes sinned. Two examples are when David counted the people of Israel, resulting in a plague attacking his nation, and after his affair with Bathsheba, resulting in the death of Uriah and his child. Several psalms specify David's situation with Bathsheba as the reason for that prayer of repentance. Psalm 51 is such a prayer, as indicated by part of the title, "A Psalm of David when Nathan the prophet went to him, after he had gone in to Bathsheba." The following verses are part of David's prayer after counting the people (2 Samuel 24).

> *10And David's heart condemned him after he had numbered the people. So David said to the Lord, "I have sinned greatly in what I have done; but now, I pray, O Lord, take away the iniquity of Your servant, for I have done very foolishly"...15So the Lord sent a plague upon Israel from the morning till the appointed time. From Dan to Beersheba seventy thousand men of the people died...17Then David spoke to the Lord when he saw the angel who was striking the people, and said, "Surely*

I have sinned, and I have done wickedly; but these sheep, what have they done? Let Your hand, I pray, be against me and against my father's house" (2 Samuel 24:10, 15, 17).

Requests for ourselves and others: Jesus' prayer in John 17 is a wonderful example of requests for ourselves and others, while giving praise to God in prayer. Some commentaries say this chapter is the real "Lord's Prayer." (Note - These are just a few points from this prayer, not a complete commentary on the chapter.

In verses 1-5, Jesus made requests for Himself. He had almost finished His work on earth and knew His crucifixion was close. He prayed that God would glorify Him as He was before He came to earth to suffer on the cross.

In verses 6-19, Jesus made requests for His disciples. Jesus had given the gospel message to them, knew that He was leaving His disciples, and prayed that God would protect them while they evangelized.

In verses 20-26, Jesus prayed for all believers. He prayed for unity and love among Christians so the world could see Jesus' love for the world and for believers to see His glory.

Thankfulness and praises to God: David's prayers of thankfulness and praise are always an example to us. 2 Samuel 22 is a prayer of praise after God delivered David from his enemies and King Saul. *The Lord is my rock and my fortress and my deliverer; The God of my strength, in whom I will trust* (verse 2b-3a). David's faith and relationship with God inspire us today! So many psalms are David's praises to God. Some verses speak of the incredible power of our almighty God and David's faith in Him.

I will both lie down in peace, and sleep; For You alone, O LORD, make me dwell in safety (Psalm 4:8).

I will praise the LORD according to His righteousness, And will sing praise to the name of the LORD Most High (Psalm 7:17).

[1]I will praise You, O Lord, with my whole heart; I will tell of all Your marvelous works. [2] I will be glad and rejoice in You; I will sing praise to Your name, O Most High (Psalm 9:1-2).

What Is Godly Meditation?

Meditation is concentrating on a specific subject or set of thoughts. Current philosophies suggest mediation increases awareness and relaxation and reduces stress.

Godly meditation is when we focus on and study God's Word to understand Him and His Word better. This meditation may make us feel more aware and relaxed with less stress. However, the real goal is to understand God, what God wants us to do, and what type of person He wants us to be.

We cannot understand God without reading what He has revealed to us through the Bible. Our meditation on what we have read enables us to understand verses more profoundly over time. Our childish understanding of a 'Bible story' should be filled with multi-layered knowledge as we think about what God wants us to know and why God put those verses in the Bible for us to study—regular meditation results in a deeper comprehension of the meatier verses. Continued meditation allows our awareness and understanding to bloom from tiny buds to gorgeous roses. Over time, these roses expand and grow more beautiful as we meditate on God and His word.

Meditation about and studying God's word prevents spiritual immaturity. A Christian cannot grow into a vital worker in God's kingdom without effort. God does not want lazy workers!

> *Be diligent to present yourself approved to God, a worker who does not need to be ashamed, rightly dividing the word of truth (2 Timothy 2:15).*

> *12For though by this time you ought to be teachers, you need someone to teach you again the first principles of the oracles of God; and you have come to need milk and not solid food. 13For everyone who partakes only of milk is unskilled in the word of righteousness, for he is a babe. 14But solid food belongs to those who are of full age, that is, those who by reason of use have their senses exercised to discern both good and evil (Hebrews 5:12-14).*

Our Prayers

Jesus often withdrew from others to pray. At other times, he prayed among his disciples and other people. His disciples thought prayer must be tricky and asked Jesus to teach them to pray as John had taught his disciples. So, how do we pray?

As a reminder, prayer is our conversation with God. One unique thing about prayer that differs from conversations with people is that prayer can be thought or spoken out loud. We can pray at any time, whether in a group, while driving down a highway, lying in our bed, or sitting on the porch. We can pray anywhere at any time. We can shout our prayers, speak our prayers, whisper our prayers, or think our prayers.

Sometimes we cannot put our concerns or emotions into words. Our situations are so big that we cannot define our feelings, needs, or circumstances in a prayer. We may be stricken or jubilant but cannot put our words into a prayer. God still hears the confusion and groaning of our souls.

> *26Likewise the Spirit also helps in our weaknesses. For we do not know what we should pray for as we ought, but the Spirit Himself makes intercession for us with groanings which cannot be uttered. 27Now He who searches the hearts knows what the mind of the Spirit is, because He makes intercession for the saints according to the will of God (Romans 8:26-27).*

God wants our conversations with Him, whether we are speaking, thinking, or groaning our prayers, alone or with others, and whether the prayers are short or long.

Our Meditation

Meditation on God and His word has always been a command from God. He wanted His people to know Him and how to be righteous in His ways. For example, He commanded Joshua and the Israelites to meditate on the Law day and night.

> [7] *Only be strong and very courageous, that you may observe to do according to all the law which Moses My servant commanded you; do not turn from it to the right hand or to the left, that you may prosper wherever you go.* [8] *This Book of the Law shall not depart from your mouth, but you shall meditate in it day and night, that you may observe to do according to all that is written in it. For then you will make your way prosperous, and then you will have good success.* [9] *Have I not commanded you? Be strong and of good courage; do not be afraid, nor be dismayed, for the Lord your God is with you wherever you go" (Joshua 1:7-9).*

God clearly wants His people to have His commandments as a priority in their minds. Deuteronomy 6 demonstrates that God's commandments are not a separate compartment of our lives, but woven into the texture of our daily activities.

> [6] *"And these words which I command you today shall be in your heart.* [7] *You shall teach them diligently to your children, and shall talk of them when you sit in your house, when you walk by the way, when you lie down, and when you rise up.* [8] *You shall bind them as a sign on your hand, and they shall be as frontlets between your eyes.* [9] *You shall write them on the doorposts of your house and on your gates (Deuteronomy 6:6-9).*

In the book of Psalms, writers show us that we can contemplate God and His commandments anywhere, at any time, and both good or bad times. A simple word search of Psalms lists these wonderful verses:

- *Psalm 1:2 - But his delight is in the law of the Lord, And in His law he meditates day and night.*
- *Psalm 4:4 - Be angry, and do not sin. Meditate within your heart on your bed, and be still. Selah*
- *Psalm 63:6 - When I remember You on my bed, I meditate on You in the night watches.*
- *Psalm 77:6 - I call to remembrance my song in the night; I meditate within my heart, And my spirit makes diligent search.*
- *Psalm 77:12 - I will also meditate on all Your work, And talk of Your deeds.*
- *Psalm 119:15 - I will meditate on Your precepts, And contemplate Your ways.*
- *Psalm 119:23 - Princes also sit and speak against me, But Your servant meditates on Your statutes.*
- *Psalm 119:27 - Make me understand the way of Your precepts; So shall I meditate on Your wonderful works.*
- *Psalm 119:48 - My hands also I will lift up to Your commandments, Which I love, And*

I will meditate on Your statutes.

- *Psalm 119:78 - Let the proud be ashamed, For they treated me wrongfully with falsehood; But I will meditate on Your precepts.*
- *Psalm 119:148 - My eyes are awake through the night watches, That I may meditate on Your word.*
- *Psalm 143:5 - I remember the days of old; I meditate on all Your works; I muse on the work of Your hands.*
- *Psalm 145:5 - I will meditate on the glorious splendor of Your majesty, And on Your wondrous works.*

Let's return to Webster's definition of meditation to consider orderly thought and conversation as a means to guide others in contemplation. We discuss and study God's word with others to improve our meditation. Learning with others adds to our understanding and helps us get deeper into God's word. Delving into the meat of the gospel feeds the rose and allows it to grow!

Meditation on God is part of how we live. As we start our day, our thoughts should include God. As we perform our tasks, our thoughts should include God. As we end our day, our thoughts should include God. God doesn't forget us; we must not forget Him. Over time and as we age, our understanding of God's word matures, because of our meditation on it. This is how we move from milk to meat of God's word.

> 8 *Finally, brethren, whatever things are true, whatever things are noble, whatever things are just, whatever things are pure, whatever things are lovely, whatever things are of good report, if there is any virtue and if there is anything praiseworthy—meditate on these things.* 9 *The things which you learned and received and heard and saw in me, these do, and the God of peace will be with you (Philippians 4:8-9).*

> 15 *Meditate on these things; give yourself entirely to them, that your progress may be evident to all.* 16 *Take heed to yourself and to the doctrine. Continue in them, for in doing this you will save both yourself and those who hear you (1 Timothy 4:15-16).*

Summary

Private time with God is essential to a Christian. Prayer to God and meditation on God and His word must be part of our daily lives. We cannot be strong workers in the kingdom without speaking to God and cannot learn how to be righteous without understanding His word. God has wanted an intimate relationship with His people since time began, and He wants such a relationship with us today.

Discussion Questions

1. What examples of prayer in the Bible move you the most?

2. When is a short prayer appropriate? A long prayer?

3. Why does God want adoration, thankfulness, and praise in a prayer?

4. What might be a confession in a prayer?

5. What type of requests might be in a prayer?

6. What other points in Jesus' prayer in John 17 might have been included in this lesson?

7. Why does the author's discussion of meditation include reading the Bible?

8. Why is meditation essential for spiritual growth?

9. How is "groaning" a prayer?

10. Why did the author have thirteen verses from Psalm about meditation in the lesson?

Apply Faith through Tangible Acts of Service and Good Works

It is common for people to feel that only faith or belief is necessary for God's salvation. Often, people quote the two following verses to prove this idea.

> *Then He said to the woman, "Your faith has saved you. Go in peace" (Luke 7:50).*

> *So they said, "Believe on the Lord Jesus Christ, and you will be saved, you and your household" (Acts 16:31).*

The verse from Luke is part of the story when a sinful woman washed Jesus' feet with her tears and hair. Jesus rebuked His host for insulting hospitality, forgave the woman's sins, and stated the woman's faith had saved her. The second verse is after the Philippian jailer asked Paul and Silas, "What must I do to be saved." They told him that belief (faith) in Jesus would save him and his family. If salvation only requires faith, why does James 2 discuss faith with works in such detail? Are works required from a Christian?

> *[14]What does it profit, my brethren, if someone says he has faith but does not have works? Can faith save him? [15]If a brother or sister is naked and destitute of daily food, [16]and one of you says to them, "Depart in peace, be warmed and filled," but you do not give them the things which are needed for the body, what does it profit? [17]Thus also faith by itself, if it does not have works, is dead. [18]But someone will say, "You have faith, and I have works." Show me your faith without your works, and I will show you my faith by my works. [19]You believe that there is one God. You do well. Even the demons believe—and tremble! [20]But do you want to know, O foolish man, that faith without works is dead? [21]Was not Abraham our father justified by works when he offered Isaac his son on the altar? [22]Do you see that faith was working together with his works, and by works faith was made perfect? [23]And the Scripture was fulfilled which says, "Abraham believed God, and it was accounted to him for righteousness." And he was called the friend of God. [24]You see then that a man is justified by works, and not by faith only. [25]Likewise, was not Rahab the harlot also justified by works when she received the messengers and sent them out another way? [26]For as the body without the spirit is dead, so faith without works is dead also (James 2:14-26).*

Notable Difference in Luke 7:50 and Acts 16:31

The notable difference in these two verses is their position in the timeline related to Christ's death, resurrection, and the establishment of the church.

The woman washed Jesus' feet before His death. Jesus forgave her sins, just as He did with the paralytic man in Matthew 9:2. Jesus was impressed by the faith of the paralytic man and his friends and said to the paralytic, "Son, be of good cheer; your sins are forgiven you," which scribes thought was blasphemous. Jesus proved to the scribes and the crowd that the Son of Man walked among them by healing the man and could forgive sins, just as He proved to Simon, who hosted the dinner, when the sinful woman washed His feet.

> [4] *But Jesus, knowing their thoughts, said, "Why do you think evil in your hearts?* [5]
> *For which is easier, to say, 'Your sins are forgiven you,' or to say, 'Arise and walk'?*
> [6] *But that you may know that the Son of Man has power on earth to forgive sins"—then He said to the paralytic, "Arise, take up your bed, and go to your house" (Matthew 9:4-6).*

Let's look at Acts 16:31 in context. First, it was after Jesus' death and resurrection, and the church with its new covenants had been established. A group of disciples, including Paul and Silas, were preaching the gospel in Philippi. This preaching of the gospel resulted in the baptism of Lydia and her household and the casting out of a spirit of divination from a slave girl. The jailer who guarded Paul and Silas in prison would have known of these activities. He had heard the gospel, believed it as truth, repented (demonstrated when he washed their stripes), and was baptized. These actions lead up to verse 34 when the jailer rejoiced, having believed in God with all his household. Why did he rejoice? He had done what he had to do to be saved according to the new gospel covenants. However, was his salvation fixed forever without other efforts from the jailer?

No, the Bible teaches that our faith saves us, but good works are also required. Good works are necessary to obey God and show our faith to the world. A Christian's works won't get them into heaven, but are the light to show the gospel to the world and to be pleasing to God. We are God's creation and were created in Christ for good works.

> *Let your light so shine before men, that they may see your good works and glorify your Father in heaven (Matthew 5:16).*

> [8] *For by grace you have been saved through faith, and that not of yourselves; it is the gift of God,* [9] *not of works, lest anyone should boast.* [10] *For we are His workmanship, created in Christ Jesus for good works, which God prepared beforehand that we should walk in them. (Ephesians 2:8-10)*

What Are Works?

In James 2, the word 'works' refers to a person's actions that are a result of faith in Jehovah God. For example, in verse 18, *But someone will say, "You have faith, and I have works." Show me your faith without your works, and I will show you my faith by my works.* In other words, works are deeds a person performs because of their faith in God and desire to please and obey Him. In the context of verse 18, a faithful believer gave clothes to naked brethren, obeyed God's command to sacrifice his son, and hid Israelite spies from guards. Their actions were a direct result of their faith in God.

God does not require great works from us. Yes, Moses led the Israelites out of Egypt, and Paul wrote at least twelve books of the New Testament (NT). However, Jesus praised the widow who gave two pennies to the temple treasury. He requires the work that we can do. We do not know which of our works will be great for someone else, nor do we always know what good works others have done, but God knows. Others can know that we are Christians by our good works.

> *Likewise, the good works of some are clearly evident, and those that are otherwise cannot be hidden (1Timothy 5:25).*

> *Even so, every good tree bears good fruit, but a bad tree bears bad fruit (Matthew 7:17).*

How Are Works Tied to Faith?

James affirmed, *"20But do you want to know, O foolish man, that faith without works is dead?" and "26For as the body without the spirit is dead, so faith without works is dead also"* (James 2:20,26). Faith without works is like a dead body. It's there, but it doesn't do anything but rot.

James went on to write about the active faith of Abraham and Rahab. Their faith affected their actions to please and obey God. *You see then that a man is justified by works, and not by faith only (James 2:24).* God requires Christians to have an active faith filled with many good works. The most clarifying verse for the relationship between faith and works is verse 22. Our works perfect our faith!

> *Do you see that faith was working together with his works, and by works faith was made perfect (James 2:22)?*

Christians are called to be different than everyone else with an active faith. How can others know of our faith if we don't show our faith with works? Our actions prove our faith to the world showing them why God is worthy of their adoration and trust.

> *14You are the light of the world. A city that is set on a hill cannot be hidden. 15 Nor do they light a lamp and put it under a basket, but on a lampstand, and it gives light to all who are in the house. 16Let your light so shine before men, that they may see your good works and glorify your Father in heaven (Matthew 5:14-16).*

Must a Christian Work to Get into Heaven?

Belief in God is not the only requirement to get into heaven. John wrote that some Pharisees believed in Jesus, but did not confess Him as they would be put out of the synagogue (John 12:42). James told us that demons believe in God and tremble (James 2:19). Saying that you believe in God is not faith, and faith without works is dead and worthless (James 2:17). Paul warns Titus against people professing to know God but have no good works demonstrating their faith.

> [15]*To the pure all things are pure, but to those who are defiled and unbelieving nothing is pure; but even their mind and conscience are defiled.* [16]*They profess to know God, but in works they deny Him, being abominable, disobedient, and disqualified for every good work (Titus 1:15-16).*

God expects more good works from those to whom He has given more, especially money. First, let me remind you that being rich is a matter of perspective, as we all are rich in something. However, God requires more from those with many blessings because they have more resources. Richness can be measured in terms of money, time, or ability, and works require work, time, effort, planning, and money. The following verses speak to those blessed with money; however, God wants us to use all our blessings for good works in His kingdom.

> [17]*Command those who are rich in this present age not to be haughty, nor to trust in uncertain riches but in the living God, who gives us richly all things to enjoy.* [18]*Let them do good, that they be rich in good works, ready to give, willing to share, 19 storing up for themselves a good foundation for the time to come, that they may lay hold on eternal life (1Timothy 6:17-19).*

At the same time, Christians should not compare their works with those of another person. We do not know everything as God does. We can only examine ourselves to see if our works are what God wants from us and are the actions that we should be taking. Remember Ephesians 2:8-10 teaches us not to boast of our good works nor will our works alone get us into heaven. Each of us must do the best work that we can.

> [3]*For if anyone thinks himself to be something, when he is nothing, he deceives himself.* [4]*But let each one examine his own work, and then he will have rejoicing in himself alone, and not in another (Galatians 6:3-4).*

Recognizing Opportunities

As stated above, God does not require great works. Very few can donate enough money to build a hospital wing, and that person may not do so with the same level of faithfulness anyway. However, all Christians can do what we can. Ordinary people can do great work in God's kingdom. Dorcas made clothes for widows (Acts 9:36-42). Barnabas sold land to support new Christians in Jerusalem (Acts 4:36-37). When we see a need, we should show up and help with that need.

What can a Christian do when they do not have money to provide clothes for widows or land to sell to provide food for other Christians? We can give of ourselves, share what we have, and show other Christians care. In other words, we do what we can! Get up from your seat and greet a visitor at church. Be friendly to that unsmiling waitress. Send a card or text to someone. Start small and build up your actions.

Watch for opportunities to serve. For example, when a friend is sick, don't just say, "Let me know if you need anything." Instead, say, "I'll bring soup to you on Tuesday," or "I'm going to the grocery store. I'll leave some crackers and ginger ale on your porch." Mow a neighbor's yard or rake their leaves. Visits are always a good work for both the sick and the healthy because it is a gift from you.

We cannot know when our small work will be seen as great by the recipient. Your words may be the only encouraging words a child hears. Your soup may be all the food in the house. Your phone call may be the only live person that has reached out to the shut-in in days. Your donated coat may warm someone who has no money to buy one. Works that don't cost you much time or money may be a huge blessing for someone else.

God has given all of us blessings. He expects us to use those blessings in His kingdom to do good works. Whatever our blessings are, we must use them! If all you have is a cup of cold water, that is what you must share. If you are blessed with more abilities and resources, you must use those for good works to obey and please God. Be a Dorcas or a Barnabas. See a need and show up!

What if No One Has Done a Good Work for Me?

A common complaint is that no one has done a good work for me or cares about me. This grumble releases no one from completing their good work! God's command for performing good works is not only for those who have received good works themselves. It is for all Christians.

A discouraged worker can use the lessons they learned when help or encouragement was not offered to them to carry out their good deeds. For example, if you have visited churches and no one greeted you, ensure visitors and those 'quiet' people receive your greeting and cheering words. If you had no encouragement during a period of confinement, give what you missed for yourself to another confined person, as you know what they need.

Don't let someone else's lack of good works stop you from performing your good works. Your faith is not their faith. Your walk with God is not theirs.

> [12]*Therefore, my beloved, as you have always obeyed, not as in my presence only, but now much more in my absence, work out your own salvation with fear and trembling;* [13]*for it is God who works in you both to will and to do for His good pleasure (Philippians 2:12-13).*

Summary

This verse is the best summary of the lesson for faithful Christians who maintain good works!

> *This is a faithful saying, and these things I want you to affirm constantly, that those who have believed in God should be careful to maintain good works. These things are good and profitable to men (Titus 3:8).*

Discussion Questions

1. If faith alone won't get us into heaven, what works are required?

2. What is the rest of the story for the Philippian jailer? Was hearing, believing, repenting, and being baptized the end of his gospel story?

3. Why is grace necessary if a Christian has faith and works?

4. Should we strive for great works or the widow's mites?

5. Why is an inactive faith like a dead body?

6. Why are works important to illustrate our faith to others?

7. Does God require more good works from some people? If so, why?

8. How can we know if a person's good work is because of their faith? Is knowing important to our faith?

9. How can we see our opportunities for a good work?

10. What if we miss opportunities for a good work? See James 2:15-16.

11. If you have seen a missed opportunity for a good work, what should you do?

12. Is a good work required every day? On a certain schedule?

13. What happens when a Christian expects good works from other Christians and does not receive them? What should the expecting Christian do?

Job Requirement # 8

Preparedness and Ability to Effectively Teach and Share Spiritual Principles

Preach the word! Be ready in season and out of season. Convince, rebuke, exhort, with all longsuffering and teaching (2 Timothy 4:2).

Probably the hardest part of being "ready to teach" is having a basic understanding of what you believe – A PhD isn't required, but a basic knowledge of your faith is required.

Too many people feel unable to teach others about the gospel and often have excuses to justify this inability. They are certain that God can see why they are unable to teach with their clear reasoning. Readers may see themselves in some of these "clear reasons" explaining why you can't teach others about your faith.

- I don't know enough Bible
- I don't have the experience to teach
- I get nervous and forget facts
- I don't have anyone to teach
- I can't speak to strangers

Yes, all of us are unique with different abilities. However, God does not accept excuses. Moses made excuses when God sent him to Pharaoh to deliver the Israelites out of Egypt and even declined God's command. Moses told God,

- I'm not good enough
- What would I say?
- They won't believe me
- They won't listen to me
- I'm not a good speaker
- Send someone else

The Bible tells us that God became angry with Moses' excuses. Moses overcame his reluctance and became one of the greatest patriarchs in the Old Testament (Exodus 3:10-4:17). Moses rose above his doubts, and we can too. We can become teachers of the gospel with study, preparation, and determination.

Preparing Yourself

The first and most important step to teaching others about the gospel is personal STUDY. Remember how you prepared for that math test in high school? You attended class, listened to the teacher, participated in class, did your homework, and studied. No one can be prepared for a math test without studying math. Preparing yourself to answer Biblical questions is not different. Christians must first study the Bible for themselves before they can effectively teach someone else.

You don't have to know everything there is to know in the Bible before you can tell someone else about the gospel. I am in my late 60s and learned new facts and Biblical relationships from recent Sunday sermons. I have read verses since my youth, but I learn new concepts about those verses today. That is how faith matures and blossoms. God does not require a full bloom of knowledge and faith before we teach. However, He does require we know the core of our faith. This core should grow as our faith matures. Regular study is involved for mastering the first principles of the gospel and for maturing to discern both good and evil.

> 12*For though by this time you ought to be teachers, you need someone to teach you again the first principles of the oracles of God; and you have come to need milk and not solid food.* 13*For everyone who partakes only of milk is unskilled in the word of righteousness, for he is a babe.* 14*But solid food belongs to those who are of full age, that is, those who by reason of use have their senses exercised to discern both good and evil (Hebrews 5:12-14).*

Early Christians did not know everything as they spread the gospel either. Some had only a basic knowledge of their faith while others had a deeper understanding of it. However, they had something special and grand and wanted to share this wonderful 'good news' with everyone they met. Luke tells us,[4] *"Therefore those who were scattered went everywhere preaching the word"* (Acts 8:4). This message of hope, promise, and salvation was eagerly shared by these new Christians, just as we should eagerly share the message today.

Overcoming Fear and Other Obstacles

A lot of people have trepidation about speaking about their faith. Others are paralyzed with the idea of leading a class. Some won't commit the time to be prepared for a study or to lead the study. All of us can find a reason to avoid teaching if we are not motivated to share our joy with others.

None of us have the same abilities as another person. Not all people are extroverts willing to talk to anyone. Not everyone has immediate recall of the information they have studied. ALL people can fulfill God's commandment to teach, no matter what our abilities are. We just have to use whatever ability we have to do the Lord's work. The style of one person's teaching is not how another person must teach.

The key to overcoming your obstacles in teaching is preparation, practice, and DOING. This author is no exception to worrying when teaching or speaking in front of a group. When I knew I had to speak to a group, my worry would begin the night before the event. While speaking, I had a red rash over my chest and neck, and I had sweaty hands. I was not comfortable! I envied those natural speakers and teachers. Still, I kept at it and became a better teacher of God's word.

Perseverance makes the most hesitant person a better teacher and speaker. The adage "Practice makes perfect" is true. Repetition makes teaching easier. God never said teaching was easy for everyone. However, He expects all of us to teach.

Recognizing Opportunities

Jesus' last commandment to us before ascending into heaven was to teach the whole world about the gospel.

> *[19]Go therefore and make disciples of all the nations, baptizing them in the name of the Father and of the Son and of the Holy Spirit, [20]teaching them to observe all things that I have commanded you; and lo, I am with you always, even to the end of the age." Amen (Matthew 28:19-20).*

Also, there are so many examples in Acts where the first-century Christians responded to adversity with joy and spread the gospel wherever they fled. At other times, they went to places where people gathered, such as the temple in Jerusalem, synagogues, or marketplaces wherever they traveled. Sometimes, discussions took place in homes among family and friends.

> *[3]As for Saul, he made havoc of the church, entering every house, and dragging off men and women, committing them to prison. [4] Therefore those who were scattered went everywhere preaching the word. [5] Then Philip went down to the city of Samaria and preached Christ to them (Acts 8:3-5).*

> *Now those who were scattered after the persecution that arose over Stephen traveled as far as Phoenicia, Cyprus, and Antioch, preaching the word to no one but the Jews only (Acts 11:19).*

Teaching every nation is commanded for all of God's disciples. Each of us must do our part to spread the gospel to all people, because God loves everyone and wants them to be saved. As Christians, we should have this same love and goal of salvation for all people.

> *This is a faithful saying and worthy of all acceptance, that Christ Jesus came into the world to save sinners, of whom I am chief (1 Timothy 1:15).*

Teaching others about Christ is not limited to Sunday School. So where are our opportunities to teach people of all nations? They are all around us! They are people you meet in everyday life - the clerks, the shoppers, and everyone else you meet. There are opportunities within our families and friends. Look for opportunities within your congregation!

You can expand your reach by supporting teachers and evangelists working across the globe. You can develop and write lessons and materials for others to use for teaching. You can provide Bibles and teaching materials for others to use. You can facilitate classes that another person leads. The limit for anyone's teaching is their imagination. We must be like the first-century Christians and teach wherever we are. Our determination should be like Isaiah's declaration, "Here am I! Send me." (Isaiah 6:8)

Teaching Methods

A great method to begin teaching is to have an "elevator speech." This is a very short talk that lasts no longer than an elevator ride. It is a good idea to have more than one idea for this speech, as it is situational. Over time, this short response to someone's question about your faith will come naturally to sow seeds in God's kingdom.

As you speak to people about your faith, you must keep in mind their perspective of faith in God. Consider how Jesus answered Nicodemus, Philip taught the Ethiopian eunuch, and Paul preached to the Athenians. You don't have to tell everything you know in a lesson; just teach from where your listener is at the time. These examples also demonstrate effective one-on-one teaching and teaching in front of a group.

- Nicodemus was a Pharisee, a teacher of the law, and a ruler among the Jews. Jesus built His lesson for Nicodemus upon the foundation of his knowledge of Jewish law and history. For example, He compared being born a Jew to being born of water and the Spirit. He allowed that He was the gateway to heaven by referencing Jacob's ladder and that He would be lifted up, as Moses' serpent to save the people. Jesus understood what Nicodemus knew and shaped His responses to that. (John 3:1-21)

- The Ethiopian was a Jewish proselyte who had been to Jerusalem to worship. He was traveling home in his chariot, reading from Isaiah 53, when Philip joined him. Philip explained how Isaiah was writing about Jesus and the gospel. Before the ride is over, the Ethiopian asked to be baptized! Because the Ethiopian was already studying the book of Isaiah, Philip used his private study to explain how Isaiah prophesied about Jesus' crucifixion and resurrection, as well as the gospel (Acts 8:26-39).

- Paul taught the Athenians differently as they had no understanding of the one true God. At that time, Athens was a center of learning, with many scholars actively seeking new ideas, and a rich city with grand temples and altars dedicated to many gods. The Athenian polytheistic culture even had altars to an Unknown God to leave no god out. So Paul started there by praising them for seeking God. He nullified the many temples and altars when he told them that gods were not made with hands and God did not live there. He acknowledged their poetry by quoting "For we are also His offspring" from Phenomena by Aratus. He closed his lesson by declaring that God will judge all men with righteousness and assured them of this promise by raising Jesus from the dead. Paul knew the logical philosophers of the city would follow this type of lesson (Acts 17:16-34).

Each of us is different and will find success in different ways.

- We can be like Aquila and Priscilla. They listened to Apollos teach, but corrected him privately about baptism (Acts 18:24-26).
- We can teach Sunday School classes at our congregation.
- We can set up personal lessons with just us and another person.
- We can lead or join group lessons. These groups can meet regularly at a restaurant before work or during lunch breaks. Groups can meet in a home. It is important to note that we must be active participants in these group discussions.

- We can be effective with impromptu discussions with people that we meet. Invite these people to worship or other studies and support them when they come.
- We can talk about the gospel with our family and friends.

No teaching method will be successful if you don't prepare yourself with personal study to understand your faith. Study ahead for a lesson that will be presented by you or someone else. Over time, you learn more yourself as you prepare to teach others! As you are teaching, someone may ask a question that you can't answer. It is all right to say, "I don't know now, but I will find out." Then study some more to find the answer!

Be diligent to present yourself approved to God, a worker who does not need to be ashamed, rightly dividing the word of truth (2 Timothy 2:15).

There are more teaching methods than can be listed in this short lesson. Colleges offer doctorate degrees in teaching methods! What Christians are commanded to do is tell others the gospel. Each of us must use our skills and abilities to teach others about God.

Teaching Materials

Of course, the Bible is the main tool anyone must use for teaching the gospel. Any other material or book that does not harmonize with the Bible doesn't conform to God's commandments and is not the truth. A person must be very familiar with their Bible to be a successful teacher and to know when supplemental materials do not follow God's word.

There are published materials that help teach others. Most of these materials are geared for specific age groups, and some are more effective than others. These include topical books, study outlines, lesson series, maps, diagrams, self-guided studies, brochures, indexes, and other teaching aids. For children, there are games and wall decorations. These materials are developed and published to support teachers of the gospel. Many gospel teachers develop their own materials. Their materials can include all the items mentioned above. Successful teachers use both published and self-developed teaching materials. Good teaching materials may help a teacher, but the Bible is the standard for using them.

No matter how good the teaching materials are, they are not effective if the teacher is not familiar with those materials. As stated earlier in this lesson, the teacher must have studied and be prepared to teach a lesson.

Preparing Others to Teach

When I was younger, I worked for the Tennessee Valley Authority (TVA). We often had classes called "Train the Trainer" to roll out a new management concept or procedure. During these classes, the attendees took the actual class with time included to prepare them to lead the class later.

Jesus prepared disciples for His departure so they could continue preaching and teaching in His absence. Often, they received upper-level courses while the crowds had basic instruction, such as an explanation of parables. He nurtured them from fishermen and tax collectors into zealous preachers of the gospel.

As we teach the world about the gospel, we must also prepare the next generation to teach. A generation without teachers could cause the world to not know Jesus and His gospel message.

Teaching and Defending Your Faith

The author isn't sure if there is a real difference between teaching and defending your faith. The knowledge, preparation, and study are the same. Both teaching and defending require courage to stand up for your faith in God. The only way the dark world can see the light of God's salvation is when we hold the gospel up for them to see.

> [14]*But even if you should suffer for righteousness' sake, you are blessed. "And do not be afraid of their threats, nor be troubled."* [15]*But sanctify the Lord God in your hearts, and always be ready to give a defense to everyone who asks you a reason for the hope that is in you, with meekness and fear (1 Peter 3:14-15).*

At times, our audience will not be receptive, but accusatory. Then, our teaching will feel more like a defense of our faith. *Only be strong and very courageous* (Joshua 1:7) while you teach and defend your faith. Sometimes, we don't get to pick our battles, but must stand up for what we believe and be brave, just as the Israelites were entering the Promised Land. Remember the hymn titled "Be Strong and Courageous" by Glenda Barnhart Schales, or at least the first verse, as you represent God and His gospel to others.

> *Verse 1:*
> *Be strong and courageous, you hosts of the Lord! Rise up for the battle, and gird on your swords! The land of His promise is yours now by right; Take all He has given; go forth to the fight!*
> *Chorus:*
> *Be strong and courageous, and conquer the foe! The Lord God is with you wherever you go!*

Summary

Christians can't retire from teaching and spreading the gospel. The Lord's work on earth is never done until Jesus comes again. There is always someone who needs to hear about God and His saving grace. Sometimes the only person to teach that person is YOU!

Discussion Questions

1. How is Moses' reluctance to lead the Israelites similar to our reluctance to teach others about the gospel? How is it different?

2. How do you know that you have mastered "the first principles of the oracles of God" and are ready to teach others?

3. What obstacles do you face when teaching others about the gospel?

4. How can we get better at recognizing opportunities to teach?

5. What is the best way to approach teaching those you know and have encountered?

6. What supplemental teaching materials do you use? How do you know these materials conform to the Bible?

7. Why is preparing others to teach important?

8. How does the song "Be Strong and Courageous" apply to the admonition in 1 Peter 3:15 to 'be ready to give a defense to everyone who asks you a reason for the hope that is in you.'

References

Hymns for Worship (Supplement), published by R.J.Stevens Music, 2007, song 22 "Be Strong and Courageous," by Glenda Barnhart Schales (music by M.W. Bassford)

Demonstrate Capacity to Promote and Maintain Peaceful Relationships in Diverse Environments

The best way to open this lesson is with a story about my mother. Open any Bible she used, and two verses will be noted on the cover pages: Philippians 4:11 and Hebrews 13:5.

> *Not that I speak in regard to need, for I have learned in whatever state I am, to be content (Philippians 4:11).*

> *Let your conduct be without covetousness; be content with such things as you have. For He Himself has said, "I will never leave you nor forsake you" (Hebrews 13:5).*

Mom did not have an easy life, but she strove to be at peace with each person in her life and to be content in whatever situation she found herself. She was an example of meekness and strength, with a strong faith in Christ Jesus and God's promises.

> *17Repay no one evil for evil. Have regard for good things in the sight of all men. 18If it is possible, as much as depends on you, live peaceably with all men (Romans 12:17-18).*

Paul admonishes the Christians in Rome to live peaceably with all men. Living peaceably with Romans was not an easy command. At that time, Christians were often the scapegoats for anything that went wrong in the Roman Empire. Also, Christians constantly lived under the threat of arrest for illegal assembly, denunciation of Caesar as a god, introduction of a new religion, and treason. A person could not be a Christian without proof of all these accusations being evident to the Romans.

Today, we Christians mostly don't live under this type of pressure. However, we must follow God's command to live peaceably with all men and to be content just as the first-century Christians were commanded. Sometimes we need to be reminded of these commandments, just as my Mom did.

Being Content

Often, we need help distinguishing between contentment and striving to better ourselves. Does contentment mean being satisfied with second best or accepting our lot in life? Not necessarily.

Think of Priscilla and Aquila. They were tentmakers in Rome when Caesar commanded all Jews to leave the city. They left Rome for Corinth, worked to make a new life, and met Paul there (Acts 18:2-3). They later traveled with Paul to Syria and stopped at Ephesus

(Acts 18:18). Priscilla and Aquila were content in all their circumstances while working as tentmakers and teaching the gospel. They did not rail against Caesar or revolt against the Roman government. They did not sit in an ash heap but strove to make a life for themselves, obeyed God, and taught the gospel.

Then and now, people want to better themselves. For example, this author was the first college graduate in her family and has changed jobs for better work environments. I went to college to learn about computers, and first-century Christians became apprentices to learn a trade. Being content is different than never working to improve your family, job, housing situation, or saving for retirement. We can work for all those things as long as God is first in our lives and not pushed to the back so we can achieve our earthly goals. Being content can be hard when the green-eyed monster called greed has overcome our contentment, making our work on earth more important to us than our devotion to God.

Paul is an excellent example of being content in all situations while working for God. Christians must lean on God in difficult conditions to be content and remember all gifts come from God when we have abundance.

> [11]*Not that I speak in regard to need, for I have learned in whatever state I am, to be content:* [12]*I know how to be abased, and I know how to abound. Everywhere and in all things I have learned both to be full and to be hungry, both to abound and to suffer need.* [13]*I can do all things through Christ who strengthens me (Philippians 4:11-13).*

We must be content in hard times. Sickness, financial distress, and cultural chaos happen to all of us. Consider Job, who lost everything, Joseph, who was sold as a slave by his brothers, and Ruth, a Moabite, who followed Naomi to Israel. All remained faithful to God, contentedly and peaceably. Think of the first-century Christians who endured incredible hardships while under Roman rule. Christian contentment does not come from being comfortable on earth. It comes from living with faith in God.

Contentment in abundance is difficult, too. Pride, greed, and covetousness can all sneak into our lives and take control. We forget God as we endeavor to acquire more and more. We depend on ourselves and not on God. Having good things is not sinful, but it can lead to discontent as we try to obtain more wealth and privilege. Remember, the rich young ruler did not follow Jesus because he loved his riches more (Matthew 19:16-22).

Living Peaceably

What is peace? According to Wikipedia, peace means societal friendship and harmony without hostility and violence. In a social sense, peace commonly means a lack of conflict (such as war) and freedom from fear of violence between individuals or groups.

Now, think of the first-century Christians living in peace with the Romans. They were often persecuted and charged with illegal assembly, denunciation of Roman Emperors as gods, introduction of a new religion, and treason.

- Groups could only assemble with a permit granted only once a month for any group. Even guild meetings had to meet this requirement.
- Emperor worship began with Julius Caesar. By the first century, it was the law for the empire to worship the Roman Emperor. Of course, Christians knew there was only one God and refused the pagan worship.
- Rome sometimes allowed its subjects to keep their religious practices, but only if Rome formally approved the religion. Rome only approved Christianity in 380 CE when Emperor Theodosius issued the Edict of Thessalonica, making Christianity the official religion (Nicene Christianity) of the Roman Empire.
- The Romans kept public order with military might and social conformity. Christian refusal to worship Roman gods and Emperors was considered treasonous.

Living peaceably in a sinful environment is HARD. Consider Shadrach, Meshach, and Abed-Nego, who were faithful Jews in King Nebuchadnezzar's court and over the affairs of the province of Babylon (Daniel 2:48-49). These men lived in a multi-theistic and cruel culture, but the king trusted them. Then King Nebuchadnezzar set up a golden statue and declared that it must be worshiped whenever certain music was played. Of course, Shadrach, Meshach, and Abed-Nego did not comply and were thrown into the fiery furnace. You know the rest of the story. Shadrach, Meshach, and Abed-Nego survived the furnace with God's assistance, stayed faithful to God, and lived peaceably among the Persians (Daniel 3:1-30).

The Christians in the first-century and the captive Jews in Babylon lived in wicked times. However, those who loved God tried to live peaceably within that culture without compromising their faith and the commandments of God. They leaned hard on God to help them, even when threatened with death for obedience to Him.

Similarly, we must live peaceably with our friends, neighbors, and families. Our light shines as we exercise the fruit of the Spirit before men. Our neighbors and family members can see how God works in our lives when we demonstrate God's love with our actions. We CAN be Christians even when our neighbors, families, and friends do not agree with, misunderstand, or do not share our faith.

> *But the fruit of the Spirit is love, joy, peace, longsuffering, kindness, goodness, faithfulness, gentleness, self-control. Against such there is no law (Galatians 5:22-23).*

Managing Our Anxiety about Our Situations

All of us worry about something – our finances, our families and friends, the state of the economy, our health, or any of a myriad of things. Some things are worthy of our attention, while other things are not. God wants us to do what we can and leave the rest in His hands. It is best to leave our constant anxiety over people and situations in God's hand through prayer. We cannot help some people, and we cannot fix some situations. In the following verses, Matthew wrote, *"Therefore do not worry about tomorrow, for tomorrow will worry about its own things. Sufficient for the day is its own trouble"* (Matthew 6:34). God knows we have troubles and is always ready to help us.

[25] "Therefore I say to you, do not worry about your life, what you will eat or what you will drink; nor about your body, what you will put on. Is not life more than food and the body more than clothing? [26] Look at the birds of the air, for they neither sow nor reap nor gather into barns; yet your heavenly Father feeds them. Are you not of more value than they? [27] Which of you by worrying can add one cubit to his stature? [28] "So why do you worry about clothing? Consider the lilies of the field, how they grow: they neither toil nor spin; [29] and yet I say to you that even Solomon in all his glory was not arrayed like one of these. [30] Now if God so clothes the grass of the field, which today is, and tomorrow is thrown into the oven, will He not much more clothe you, O you of little faith? [31] "Therefore do not worry, saying, 'What shall we eat?' or 'What shall we drink?' or 'What shall we wear?' [32] For after all these things the Gentiles seek. For your heavenly Father knows that you need all these things. [33] But seek first the kingdom of God and His righteousness, and all these things shall be added to you. [34] Therefore do not worry about tomorrow, for tomorrow will worry about its own things. Sufficient for the day is its own trouble (Matthew 6:25-34).

We cannot be content and live peaceably without God's help. The troubles in our lives are too overwhelming for us to continue without Him. Our faith must be strong so that we can lean on God as we navigate through earthly problems and tribulations.

[5b] The Lord is at hand. [6] Be anxious for nothing, but in everything by prayer and supplication, with thanksgiving, let your requests be made known to God; [7] and the peace of God, which surpasses all understanding, will guard your hearts and minds through Christ Jesus. (Philippians 4:5b-7)

Others can see Christ in us when we live contentedly and peacefully with those around us. We bring honor to Christ when we are productive workers in our lives and God's kingdom. *"Let your requests be made known to God."* Pray! Then pray some more. Draw near to God and share your worries and anxieties with Him (even clinical anxieties). Look for God in your life and count the blessings He has given you.

[11] that you also aspire to lead a quiet life, to mind your own business, and to work with your own hands, as we commanded you, [12] that you may walk properly toward those who are outside, and that you may lack nothing (1 Thessalonians 4:11-12).

Be the person you want others to be. Let God guide you to properly walk as a Christian. Walk is an active verb with the intent of a goal. God has set goals for us to live quietly, minding our own business, and working. Let God fill your life and mind so that contentment fills your heart.

Anger

We all get angry at times, which is not necessarily a sin. Remember, Jesus got angry and drove the money changers and sellers out of the temple (John 2:13-16).

"Be angry, and do not sin": do not let the sun go down on your wrath (Ephesians 4:26).

Even the most content and peaceable living person will get angry at times. Moses got angry at the complaining of the Israelites. He let his anger control him, was not obedient to God, and sinned. He paid a price for his sinful anger and was not allowed to enter the Promised Land. This example of Moses' sinful outrage shows us that our anger must not overcome us and lead us to sinful thoughts or behavior.

Anger can pop up as we strive to be content and live peaceably with others. We get angry because the kids continue to leave chores undone, our nation passes laws with which we disagree, nations or groups of people war against one another, or our neighbors gossip about us. Living peaceably among others does not mean issues won't arise.

The concern is how we handle those issues. "What would Jesus do?" This slogan is good to remember as we learn to control our anger. Managing anger with contentment can be a dichotomy for us; each situation is different. The author's best advice is to avoid sinful anger and move back into contentment. One answer will not fit every situation

Our Peace with God

When we live peaceably with men and are content in our hearts, our peace with God is immense. Harmony with God is the most important peace that anyone can have. There will always be war, threats of war (Matthew 24:6), disease, and sadness on earth. Peace among all men on earth is not promised to us, as the earth is a broken place. However, God promises peace with Him through Jesus.

> [5]*Let your gentleness be known to all men. The Lord is at hand.* [6]*Be anxious for nothing, but in everything by prayer and supplication, with thanksgiving, let your requests be made known to God;* [7] *and the peace of God, which surpasses all understanding, will guard your hearts and minds through Christ Jesus (Philippians 4:5-7).*

God wants us to handle our worries by praying and counting our blessings, as He is always with us.

> [17]*But the wisdom that is from above is first pure, then peaceable, gentle, willing to yield, full of mercy and good fruits, without partiality and without hypocrisy.* [18]*Now the fruit of righteousness is sown in peace by those who make peace (James 3:17-18).*

Summary

God commands us to be content with our lives and to live in peace with others. He is with us during our good and bad times and wants us to use prayer to put our troubles on Him. A quiet life allows us to shine our light in this world and show others how faith in God overcomes all tribulations. Prayer is always a tool to help us manage our anxieties about earthly situations.

Discussion Questions

1. What can we learn from the Roman persecutions of Christians?

2. How are Priscilla and Aquila examples of contentment?

3. How can we be content when we have a deadly health diagnosis or when our country is at war?

4. Why didn't the first-century Christians work to overthrow the evil Roman Empire?

5. How could the Jews remain faithful to God while captives in Babylon?

6. How is the fruit of the Spirit helpful for contentment and living peaceably among others?

7. Why must we be careful about our anxiety?

8. What does Philippians 4 say about managing our anxiety and worries?

9. What does 1 Thessalonians 4:12 mean when the verse says, "that you may lack nothing?"

10. What advice do you have for managing anger?

11. What is the difference between peace with God and peace with men? How does peace with God help with our contentment and peace with men?

12. How can we be content and live peaceably within our congregations?

13. Must our personal contentment and peaceable living accept social ideas that God has condemned? How do we manage that?

Exemplary Control Over Spoken Communication, Including Respectful, Truthful, and Edifying Speech

The third chapter in the book of James has many warnings about the dangers of our tongues (speech). James writes, *"The tongue is a fire, a world of iniquity. The tongue is so set among our members that it defiles the whole body, and sets on fire the course of nature; it is set on fire by hell" (James 3:6).* He even warns us, *"No man can tame the tongue. It is an unruly evil, full of deadly poison"* (James 3:8).

If the tongue is so evil, why don't we cut it out to eliminate all the insurmountable problems that it causes? Why did God create mankind with such an evil member? We don't cut our tongues out because God made them. God did not make our tongues for evil but for good. We must control our speech and use our tongues for good in God's kingdom.

So, how can our tongues be useful in the kingdom? We can use our tongues to praise God, teach about God, express love, correct others, explain our faith, and so many other useful ways!

Praising God

One way to use our speech for good is to praise God. All our prayers should include praise to God, but praise to God must be a part of our daily life, too. Before we praise God, we must be aware of what God has done for us. After all, how can we appreciate what God has done and will do for us if we are unaware of God's blessings? Giving praise to God makes us think and speak of all the glories, wonders, and faithfulness of our God.

> *Therefore by Him let us continually offer the sacrifice of praise to God, that is, the fruit of our lips, giving thanks to His name (Hebrews 13:15).*

Hebrews 13:15 commands offering the sacrifice of praise to God and calls this sacrifice the fruit of our lips! Words ought to be easy for us, but we often stop praising God in front of others and don't know what to say in our prayers. One idea that might make this easier is to keep a written list of things God has done for you, your family, your community, your state, your country, the world, and—well, you get the idea. It's like the song. Counting and naming your blessings will surprise you with all God has done. We must be aware of His gifts to us and praise Him for them.

Teaching about God

What would Jesus do? This question became a famous slogan; many wore colorful plastic bracelets engraved with the slogan or its abbreviation—WWJD. However, in keeping with the slogan, let the author assure you that Jesus would teach others about God and the gospel with compassion and love. Even His last words to His disciples stressed the importance of teaching others the gospel.

> *Then Jesus went about all the cities and villages, teaching in their synagogues, preaching the gospel of the kingdom, and healing every sickness and every disease among the people (Matthew 9:35).*

> *Go into all the world and preach the gospel to every creature (Mark 16:15b).*

> [19]*Go therefore and make disciples of all the nations, baptizing them in the name of the Father and of the Son and of the Holy Spirit,* [20]*teaching them to observe all things that I have commanded you (Matt 28:19-20a).*

It is easy to feel that we, as individuals, cannot make many ripples in this world's pond. The pond is so big, and we are only one person. Nothing could be farther from the truth. Paul turned "the world upside down" with his gospel teaching in Thessalonica (Acts 17:6). Big ripples indeed! He is a wonderful example of the impact that one person can have. For example, Paul taught Caesar's household while he was jailed (Phil. 4:22), Lydia's household on a Sabbath morning (Acts 16:15), Athenian philosophers after seeing the altar of the Unknown God (Acts 17:22ff), and Roman officials in Caesarea (Acts 23-25). Paul just taught people about God and the gospel wherever he was. He made whatever his situation was into a teaching situation.

Teaching Our Children

The gospel is one generation away from apostasy when Christians don't teach the children. We cannot transfer our faith to them, as they must have their own faith.

In Deuteronomy 6, we are told, [4]*"Hear, O Israel: The Lord our God, the Lord is one!* [5]*You shall love the Lord your God with all your heart, with all your soul, and with all your strength.* [6]*"And these words which I command you today shall be in your heart.* [7]*You shall teach them diligently to your children, and shall talk of them when you sit in your house, when you walk by the way, when you lie down, and when you rise up."*

We must use our tongues to teach children about our love of God, His love for us, and His commandments for righteous living. Our love for our children causes us to want all good things for them, and the best thing for them is faith in God.

Expressing Love and Affection

The New Testament tells all Christians to love one another throughout its pages. An online search of it using only the words "love one another" yielded 22 results. However, those verses don't use any words referring to speaking. We only need to read the salutations of Paul's epistles to see his words express affection from and to the mentioned Christians. Speech that is kind, encouraging, and sometimes correcting is part of loving one another. The parable of the prodigal son beautifully shows us a father expressing love for his lost son and correcting another son.

> [20]*"And he arose and came to his father. But when he was still a great way off, his father saw him and had compassion, and ran and fell on his neck and kissed him. [21]And the son said to him, 'Father, I have sinned against heaven and in your sight, and am no longer worthy to be called your son.' [22]"But the father said to his servants, 'Bring out the best robe and put it on him, and put a ring on his hand and sandals on his feet. [23]And bring the fatted calf here and kill it, and let us eat and be merry; [24]for this my son was dead and is alive again; he was lost and is found.' And they began to be merry (Luke 15:20-24).*

> [31]*"And he said to him, 'Son, you are always with me, and all that I have is yours. [32]It was right that we should make merry and be glad, for your brother was dead and is alive again, and was lost and is found'" (Luke 15:31-32).*

Christians are to love one another and express that love in word and deed. This care is for our families, friends, community, country, and people all over the world. God loves all those people, and we must, too. As the prodigal son's father expressed love in word and deed to both the straying and faithful son, so must we.

Correcting Others

We all have heard people say falsehoods and half-truths about God. At least, we think it wasn't true. Before we can correct anyone, we must know what the Bible says ourselves. Unfortunately, we cannot take a knowledge pill to become an expert, and we cannot correct anyone if we aren't sure of the truth. That means personal study is required! We must know what God said about the issue before we can correct anyone. Armed with solid knowledge of the problem, we must consider how to address it with the person(s). Talking louder or quoting more Bible verses than the other person does not win the argument or teach the other person.

The story of Priscilla, Aquila, and Apollos is an excellent example of how to approach someone who is teaching incorrectly.

> [24]*Now a certain Jew named Apollos, born at Alexandria, an eloquent man and mighty in the Scriptures, came to Ephesus. [25]This man had been instructed in the way of the Lord; and being fervent in spirit, he spoke and taught accurately the things of the Lord, though he knew only the baptism of John. [26]So he began to speak boldly in the synagogue. When Aquila and Priscilla heard him, they took him aside and explained to him the way of God more accurately. (Acts 18:24-26)*

Aquila and Priscilla did not have a public feud with Apollos, but took him aside and taught him about baptism. Apollos, then, became an even more effective worker in God's kingdom.

One of my favorite personal stories is how one of my young sons corrected a preacher. We were visiting a small church in the Tennessee mountains. The preacher used the story of the ten spies in his sermon and kept getting the number of spies wrong. My son squirmed more in the pew each time the preacher said the wrong number, but he didn't make a scene during the sermon. However, as we walked out the front door, he quietly told the preacher which number of spies did what. A child correcting the preacher! The child knew what the Bible said and taught the older man with sureness and kindness. If a child can correct an authority figure, then you can too.

Remember, the gospel allows Christians many liberties, and our depth of understanding blooms over time. Discussing issues in this area requires acknowledging those liberties and deepening our understanding. For example, my daughter-in-law told me she had studied biblical passages related to nakedness due to a conversation with a friend that changed her ideas about modesty. I had never considered nakedness in the Bible! She was deepening her understanding of the Bible and certainly added to mine. She understood the importance of studying and discussing the gospel with an open mind.

Quietly handling incorrect teaching works most of the time, but not every time. Remember to be like Jesus as you teach, not a shouting, mad person. Sometimes, people will not listen to us or are unavailable to discuss with us. We must handle each situation the best we can. We could repeat our 'lessons' for several years before the person listens, or we write letters and emails to the unavailable person. There is no set script. Sometimes, we must shake the dust from our feet as the apostles did. We can use our speech in God's kingdom to correct another person about God's word, but not always with success.

Explaining Our Faith

1 Peter urges us to be prepared to defend our faith. Many Christians may find it easier to go with the flow, but we must consider how to articulate our faith to others.

> *But sanctify the Lord God in your hearts, and always be ready to give a defense to everyone who asks you a reason for the hope that is in you, with meekness and fear (1 Peter 3:15).*

Let's look at the different parts of this verse.

- Sanctify God
  Sanctify means to declare holy and revere. It is crucial that we understand and acknowledge that God must be first in everything to us as the Most Holy God.

- Ready to defend
  If someone called you in front of a judge about unpaid bills, you would come in front of that judge with proof of the bill and how you paid it. You would not be unconcerned or casual about your defense in front of the judge. Christians are commanded to be as prepared to defend their faith and hope in God. How can we teach others about the gospel if we don't know why we believe or what we be-

lieve? Our responses to others must be rational and clear. We cannot defend the reason for the hope in us if we do not know that reason!

- Meekness and fear
  Meekness means we are gentle with the people we discuss the gospel with. Meekness has nothing to do with our strength when teaching others. It means that we don't talk over them, shout at them, or make fun of them. Meekness is hard, but remember that Jesus was meek. Fear does not mean being scared or afraid in this context, but it is reverence for the subject. We don't want to be misunderstood, give the wrong answer, or not know an answer. Our fear or reverence for God is essential in explaining to others why we believe the gospel message.

Strength and courage are required to defend our faith and hope in God. Think about Peter and John in front of the Sanhedrin Council. *"We ought to obey God rather than men"* (Acts 5:29). Think about Shadrach, Meshach, and Abednego when entering the fiery furnace. [17]*"If that is the case, our God whom we serve is able to deliver us from the burning fiery furnace, and He will deliver us from your hand, O king.* [18]*But if not, let it be known to you, O king, that we do not serve your gods, nor will we worship the gold image which you have set up"* (Daniel 3:17-18). We must be as strong and courageous and able to defend our faith.

Other Useful Ways

Our daily lives offer many opportunities to speak about God and uplift others. Ephesians 4:29 teaches us to think before speaking and use our words as Jesus would have.

> [29]*Do not let any unwholesome talk come out of your mouths, but only what is helpful for building others up according to their needs, that it may benefit those who listen.* [30]*And do not grieve the Holy Spirit of God, with whom you were sealed for the day of redemption.* [31]*Get rid of all bitterness, rage and anger, brawling and slander, along with every form of malice.* [32]*Be kind and compassionate to one another, forgiving each other, just as in Christ God forgave you (Eph 4:29-32).*

Our words should be uplifting without unwholesomeness, bitterness, rage, anger, fighting, slander, or malice. Thoughtless words can sever ties between a person and God. Your words are important. Let them be kind, compassionate, and forgiving, even under challenging circumstances. Think of Jesus' kind words on the cross to the thief beside him and John about His mother. His caring words gave them hope during those dark hours.

Similarly, our words can give others hope when they are struggling, and a canned speech isn't enough. A child who is bullied has different needs than someone who has lost their job. Think before you speak! Don't tell the child to toughen up, but provide real help. Don't tell the job seeker that something will turn up, offer to help with babysitting during interviews or a connection to your home internet. Pray for all of them! Don't be stingy with your words when asking God to help others.

Summary

The book of James warns Christians that words can be evil and harmful. However, the New Testament also teaches us how to use our words for good in God's kingdom. With study and practice, anyone can use their words to praise God, teach about God, express love, correct others, explain our faith, and many other ways.

Discussion Questions

1. Why is James so adamant about the evils of the tongue?

2. How can we improve our praise to God? Is improvement essential?

3. Why does the author assure us that Jesus taught with compassion and love?

4. How can we be like Paul and turn our situation into a teaching situation?

5. How can apostasy be related to teaching children?

6. How can we express love for one another without using the words "I love you?"

7. How can you have an evolving understanding of a Bible issue over time? Think about issues involving our liberties for this question.

8. How can you correct a person who is sure of their righteousness?

9. How are we required to defend our faith today?

10. How can our words build someone up according to their needs?

11. What are other ways that we can use our speech for good in God's kingdom?

Strong Discernment and Sound Judgment in Moral, Ethical, and Spiritual Matters

We have all heard that the Bible says we cannot judge others. This text in Matthew 7, which is part of the Sermon on the Mount, is often the basis for this saying.

> *[1]"Judge not, that you be not judged. [2]For with what judgment you judge, you will be judged; and with the measure you use, it will be measured back to you (Matthew 7:1-2).*

"Do not judge" is an unambiguous phrase. Are Christians commanded never to judge anything or anyone? Before answering this question, consider the verses before and after this text to see Jesus' teaching in context. During the Sermon on the Mount, Jesus taught His followers to live righteous lives. For example, six times He said, "You have heard that it was said" or "it has been said" referring to a tradition or Pharisaical practice. Then, He taught them how His followers would live. The verses immediately following Matthew 7:1-2 teach us to judge ourselves before we consider the faults of others, which is how He wants us to live. Using our judgment is part of a righteous life.

> *[3]And why do you look at the speck in your brother's eye, but do not consider the plank in your own eye? [4]Or how can you say to your brother, 'Let me remove the speck from your eye'; and look, a plank is in your own eye? [5]Hypocrite! First remove the plank from your own eye, and then you will see clearly to remove the speck from your brother's eye (Matthew 7:3-5).*

Christian judgment is often depicted as a preacher yelling damnation from the pulpit and assuring his listeners they are going to hell. The author will not say this is unnecessary, but thinks it is generally ineffective. Daily, we must use our judgment to discern between the good and evil of our lives and not only declare hell from the pulpit. Judgment and discernment are constant for a Christian as we apply God's word and live as He commands.

What Is Judgment?

Often, Christians jump to God's final judgment for a Biblical definition of the word judgment, which is not the definition or part of this lesson. God's judgment is not the same as our judgment. Yes, we often perceive how God would judge a person (good and bad), but we are not correct every time, and that type of judgment is not our job.

> *[24]Some men's sins are clearly evident, preceding them to judgment, but those of some men follow later. [25]Likewise, the good works of some are clearly evident, and those that are otherwise cannot be hidden (1Timothy 5:24-25).*

Oxford Dictionary defines judgment as "the ability to make considered decisions or come to sensible conclusions." Christians must make considered decisions with sensible conclusions daily. We judge when we participate in social events, buy clothes, raise our children, involve ourselves in social media, or interact with strangers in a store. We do not have to preside over a courtroom to judge. However, we need to know and understand God's law to judge and make sensible conclusions correctly, just as a federal judge must know our nation's laws.

What Is Discernment?

Oxford Dictionary has two definitions for discernment.

1. The ability to judge well.
2. (In Christian contexts) Perception in the absence of judgment with a view to obtaining spiritual guidance and understanding.

The author has often heard the introductory verse "Do not judge" explained this way. "Christians are not to judge, but discern." This explanation is not all of the truth. Discernment is our ability to recognize how God's righteousness applies to the situation and judge well. In the end, we must judge. However, before judging, we must first understand the details of the person or situation and apply God's commandments and guidance. This is discernment.

Discernment must come before judging a situation or person. Discernment has been praised and sought after by righteous people throughout time. For example,

> *Then Pharaoh said to Joseph, "Inasmuch as God has shown you all this, there is no one as discerning and wise as you (Genesis 41:39).*

> *[8]And Your servant is in the midst of Your people whom You have chosen, a great people, too numerous to be numbered or counted. [9]Therefore give to Your servant an understanding heart to judge Your people, that I may discern between good and evil. For who is able to judge this great people of Yours?" [10]The speech pleased the Lord, that Solomon had asked this thing (1 Kings 3:8-10).*

> *[9]And this I pray, that your love may abound still more and more in knowledge and all discernment, [10]that you may approve the things that are excellent, that you may be sincere and without offense till the day of Christ, [11]being filled with the fruits of righteousness which are by Jesus Christ, to the glory and praise of God (Philippians 1:9-11).*

Criterion for Judgment and Discernment

Just as a federal judge must know the nation's laws to judge and discern, we must know God's law. In Paul's letter to the Philippians, he advised them to grow in knowledge and discernment so they could know the excellence and righteousness that comes through Jesus.

[9]And this I pray, that your love may abound still more and more in knowledge and all discernment, [10] that you may approve the things that are excellent, that you may be sincere and without offense till the day of Christ, 11 being filled with the fruits of righteousness which are by Jesus Christ, to the glory and praise of God (Philippians 1:9-11).

This knowledge is an absolute necessity! We cannot distinguish between good and evil and choose the things that are excellent, if we don't know God's law and His righteousness. We cannot know if things or situations labeled as righteous here on earth are labeled correctly if we cannot recognize how God has defined righteousness. Knowledge of God's law does not come by osmosis but requires effort. Just reading your Bible is not enough. Every reader must absorb and think about the words in their Bible with discernment to develop wisdom and apply them in life.

Be diligent to present yourself approved to God, a worker who does not need to be ashamed, rightly dividing the word of truth (2 Timothy 2:15).

Maturity

We grow and mature from babies to adults as we study and ponder God's word. Adding to our knowledge and understanding is a constant undertaking as we live righteous lives. We are spiritually immature if we do not continuously develop within God's word and cannot correctly discern between good and evil in our lives.

[12]For though by this time you ought to be teachers, you need someone to teach you again the first principles of the oracles of God; and you have come to need milk and not solid food. [13]For everyone who partakes only of milk is unskilled in the word of righteousness, for he is a babe. [14]But solid food belongs to those who are of full age, that is, those who by reason of use have their senses exercised to discern both good and evil (Hebrews 5:12-14).

[1]Therefore, laying aside all malice, all deceit, hypocrisy, envy, and all evil speaking, [2]as newborn babes, desire the pure milk of the word, that you may grow thereby, [3]if indeed you have tasted that the Lord is gracious (1 Peter 2:1-3).

Maturity will look different for each of us as God's word continues to bloom over our lifetime. For example, the meaning of a particular verse will get deeper or have a different application for you over time. This growth cannot happen if group and individual study of God's word are not part of your life. Without continuous study and spiritual growth, maturity is stunted, and discernment between good and evil is impossible.

Christian Liberties

The first-century discussion of eating meat offered to idols is a good example of maturity within Christian liberties. At that time, meat for sale in markets often had first been offered to a temple god. Many first-century Christians thought that buying and eating that meat was supporting that temple god and slighting the one true God. Others thought marketplace meat was just meat. The New Testament has no direct command to avoid such meat, and each person had to decide whether or not such meat was a proper food.

Each Christian had to decide how eating offerings to a false god affected their communion with God. If eating the meat was supporting a temple god, then it was sinful to eat the meat. If eating the meat had nothing to do with the temple god, then it was not sinful for the Christian to enjoy the meat. Marketplace meat was a major discussion during the first century! These Christians did not want to sin or appear to support an idol. Note that each Christian must allow other Christians to have their opinion on the matter of meat and seeking to make it sinful was not encouraged.

> *It is good neither to eat meat nor drink wine nor do anything by which your brother stumbles or is offended or is made weak (Romans 14:21).*

> *Therefore, if food makes my brother stumble, I will never again eat meat, lest I make my brother stumble (1 Corinthians 8:13).*

> *Eat whatever is sold in the meat market, asking no questions for conscience' sake (1 Corinthians 10:25).*

Eating the marketplace meat was each Christian's choice as they discerned God's law. The Christians' understanding of idol-offered meat might change over time, and God allows that to happen, too. God desires us to help each other grow in knowledge and discernment with mercy and love.

> [12]So speak and so do as those who will be judged by the law of liberty. [13]For judgment is without mercy to the one who has shown no mercy. Mercy triumphs over judgment (James 2:12-13).

Judging Your Brother

Let's go back to the introduction of this lesson about judging other people. So, Christians don't judge others or don't judge them until you have judged yourself? Verses in James 4 have clear warnings about judging your brother.

> *[11]Do not speak evil of one another, brethren. He who speaks evil of a brother and judges his brother, speaks evil of the law and judges the law. But if you judge the law, you are not a doer of the law but a judge. [12]There is one Lawgiver, who is able to save and to destroy. Who are you to judge another (James 4:11-12)?*

In these verses, James talks explicitly about someone who acts as an authoritative judge of Christ's law and makes a final judgment of another. This type of judging is NOT a Christian's job. James Coffman explains it this way in his commentary on Matthew 7:1: *"Making a private, personal, and tentative appraisal of others is not forbidden; but 'judging' is prohibited. Only Jesus Christ can judge in that manner."*

> [30]*Truly, these times of ignorance God overlooked, but now commands all men everywhere to repent,* [31]*because He has appointed a day on which He will judge the world in righteousness by the Man whom He has ordained. He has given assurance of this to all by raising Him from the dead"(Acts 17:30-31).*

> *I charge you therefore before God and the Lord Jesus Christ, who will judge the living and the dead at His appearing and His kingdom: (2 Timothy 4:1)*

While Jesus walked on earth, He did not act as the authoritative judge of His law, as it was not the proper time. Jesus came to teach and save the world. He knew His time as a man was not to be the final judge but to die to save us. He used His discernment to judge evil on earth, such as the moneychangers in the temple, which is not the same as someone's final judgment.

> [47]*And if anyone hears My words and does not believe, I do not judge him; for I did not come to judge the world but to save the world.* [48]*He who rejects Me, and does not receive My words, has that which judges him—the word that I have spoken will judge him in the last day (John 12:47-48).*

Yes, we make judgments of others. Righteous people use Christ's law as their measuring stick to discern between good and evil. However, Christians can never make the final judgment of another, as only Christ can do that. We cannot decide whether salvation is due to someone else or not!

> [1]*Let a man so consider us, as servants of Christ and stewards of the mysteries of God.* [2]*Moreover it is required in stewards that one be found faithful.* [3]*But with me it is a very small thing that I should be judged by you or by a human court. In fact, I do not even judge myself.* [4]*For I know of nothing against myself, yet I am not justified by this; but He who judges me is the Lord.* [5]*Therefore judge nothing before the time, until the Lord comes, who will both bring to light the hidden things of darkness and reveal the counsels of the hearts. Then each one's praise will come from God (1 Corinthians 4:1-5).*

Attitude for Judgment and Discernment

A Christian constantly makes judgments and discerns people, places, and events. First, we must know Christ's Law to use as our measuring stick, to judge ourselves first, and never act as the final authority in our judgments. However, our attitude is also essential.

> *And be kind to one another, tenderhearted, forgiving one another, even as God in Christ forgave you (Eph 4:32).*

Jesus was kind to people who followed Him, hoping for free food (Mark 6:30-44). He was kind to Peter, who sank into the water as his faith wavered (Matthew 14:22-33). He was kind to the two thieves on crosses beside Him (Luke 23:39-43). We must be like Jesus and be kind, tenderhearted, and forgiving.

The Lord's Body

We cannot leave a discussion of discernment without discussing 1 Corinthians 11:29, a commandment to discern the Lord's body.

> *For he who eats and drinks in an unworthy manner eats and drinks judgment to himself, not discerning the Lord's body (1 Corinthians 11:29).*

This verse speaks of our final judgment (salvation or damnation) and is essential to understand. Whether the verse speaks of Jesus' physical body or His spiritual body (the church) does not minimize the warning. Jesus knowingly gave His physical body as a sacrifice for our sins. He foreknew the degradation, pain, and anguish this sacrifice would mean for Him, yet He did it. Jesus loved even those of us not yet born and died to give us salvation. He chose to save us.

The church is Jesus' spiritual body on earth, comprised of people united with Him through baptism. Earlier in chapter 11, Paul asked the Corinthians if they despised the church (verse 22) because they were not sharing their meals with Christians who had no food. As we share the Lord's Supper, Christians cannot disregard the Lord's spiritual body.

Look at this verse in context for more ideas of the teaching in it, especially verse 31.

> 27*Therefore whoever eats this bread or drinks this cup of the Lord in an unworthy*
> *manner will be guilty of the body and blood of the Lord.* 28*But let a man exam-*
> *ine himself, and so let him eat of the bread and drink of the cup.* 29*For he who*
> *eats and drinks in an unworthy manner eats and drinks judgment to himself, not*
> *discerning the Lord's body.* 30*For this reason many are weak and sick among*
> *you, and many sleep.* 31*For if we would judge ourselves, we would not be judged.*
> 32*But when we are judged, we are chastened by the Lord, that we may not be*
> *condemned with the world (1 Corinthians 11:27-32).*

Examine yourself! Christians are to judge themselves first. Christ died for each of us. If we examine and judge ourselves first for sin and areas of improvement, He will not have died in vain.

Summary

We cannot condemn anyone to hell or award heaven either; that is Christ's job. However, Christians use judgment and discernment daily to decide between good and evil. Proper discernment requires knowledge of Christ's law, maturity, and kindness. Discernment is also needed as we share the Lord's Supper.

Discussion Questions

1. Is Matthew 7:1-2 a teaching or a commandment?

2. Why is knowledge required to judge correctly? What knowledge should a Christian pursue?

3. If discernment means "judging well," how can a Christian discern?

4. How can we know if we are "rightly dividing the word of truth?"

5. Do you have an example of how your understanding of a text changed as you matured as a Christian?

6. Why is it hard not to judge when Christian liberties are involved?

7. Discuss the balance between a personal appraisal of someone or something and "judging."

8. Why is kindness and forgiveness part of judging and discernment?

9. List some ideas to successfully "discern the Lord's body."

Consistent Display of Hope, Personal Holiness, and Moral Integrity in Daily Conduct

And when he had found him, he brought him to Antioch. So it was that for a whole year they assembled with the church and taught a great many people. And the disciples were first called Christians in Antioch (Acts 11:26).

Then He commanded His disciples that they should tell no one that He was Jesus the Christ (Matthew 16:20).

The beginning of the gospel of Jesus Christ, the Son of God (Mark 1:1).

Acts 11:26 teaches us Jesus' followers were first called Christians in Antioch. Jesus had the title of and was the Christ, which means "the anointed one." Over time, this title of Christ became part of Jesus' name to His followers, and they began to be called by His name.

Agrippa recognized this affiliation when he said, *"You almost persuade me to become a Christian"* (Acts 26:28). Peter also acknowledged the name of Christ's followers when he was encouraging them in their trials in 1 Peter 4:16, *"Yet if anyone suffers as a Christian, let him not be ashamed, but let him glorify God in this matter."*

Christians must always consider whose name they wear and what this name represents to others. Sometimes, our actions are the loudest gospel lesson a nonbeliever will hear. A line in the song "Dear Lord, Hear My Prayer" by Carri Mullins Hawkins must be our motto, *"To live for Christ whose name I wear."* Christians must live as Jesus would have us live, with hope and holiness.

What Is Hope?

Christian hope is the certain conviction and trust that the Bible is true and God will keep all the promises He made in it. This certainty brings Christians joy, peace, and perseverance in the present time. This hope sustains Christians during the trials of our earthly lives as we look forward to our eternal one.

Now may the God of hope fill you with all joy and peace in believing, that you may abound in hope by the power of the Holy Spirit (Romans 15:13).

3 And not only that, but we also glory in tribulations, knowing that tribulation produces perseverance; 4 and perseverance, character; and character, hope. 5 Now hope does not disappoint, because the love of God has been poured out in our hearts by the Holy Spirit who was given to us (Romans 5:3-5).

For What Are We Hoping

Our most basic hope is that Christ has physically risen from the dead, and we will see a similar resurrection. Christians cannot be saved from their sins without Jesus' death and resurrection. We receive grace because Jesus died for our sins.

> *[17]And if Christ is not risen, your faith is futile; you are still in your sins! [18]Then also those who have fallen asleep in Christ have perished. [19]If in this life only we have hope in Christ, we are of all men the most pitiable (1 Corinthians 15:17-19).*

> *So that as sin reigned in death, even so grace might reign through righteousness to eternal life through Jesus Christ our Lord (Romans 5:21).*

Our basic hope leads to the hope of eternal life and glory with God. Paul writes about this hope in his letter to Titus because God is faithful in keeping all His promises. Christians are blessed that God's mysteries have been revealed in the gospel so that we can have hope in all God's promises.

> *In hope of eternal life which God, who cannot lie, promised before time began (Titus 1:2).*

> *That having been justified by His grace we should become heirs according to the hope of eternal life (Titus 3:7).*

> *[26]The mystery which has been hidden from ages and from generations, but now has been revealed to His saints. [27]To them God willed to make known what are the riches of the glory of this mystery among the Gentiles: which is Christ in you, the hope of glory (Colossians 1:26-27).*

Examples of Hope

God had promised Abraham that all nations would be blessed through his seed. Do you remember that Abraham and Sarah were very old at the time of this promise? Fertility for both of them was considered "dead" due to their age. However, Abraham did not waver in his belief that God would keep this promise. He had certain conviction and trust (which is hope) that God was faithful in every word coming from His mouth.

> *[17](As it is written, "I have made you a father of many nations") in the presence of Him whom he believed—God, who gives life to the dead and calls those things which do not exist as though they did; [18]who, contrary to hope, in hope believed, so that he became the father of many nations, according to what was spoken, "So shall your descendants be" (Romans 4:17-18).*

Paul repeatedly preached God's promises, hope in Christ's resurrection, and eternal life in heaven. A time that comes to mind is his speech before King Agrippa and Bernice. This important political event for Caesarea's dignitaries was well attended with much pomp. Still, Paul was strong in his conviction of God's promises. He told King Agrippa, "[6]*And now I stand and am judged for the hope of the promise made by God to our fathers.* [7]*To this promise our twelve tribes, earnestly serving God night and day, hope to attain. For this hope's sake, King Agrippa, I am accused by the Jews.* [8]*Why should it be thought incredible by you that God raises the dead?" (Acts 26:6-8).* Paul continued his defense before Agrippa and then concluded, "[25]*I am not mad, most noble Festus, but speak the words of truth and reason.* [26]*For the king, before whom I also speak freely, knows these things; for I am convinced that none of these things escapes his attention, since this thing was not done in a corner"* (Acts 26:25-26). Paul's hope in God's promises carried him through this day.

Our Hope

Our hope is different than the hope of our Old Testament heroes. They did not have the full gospel revealed to them as it is to us about the resurrection of Christ. Their hope was based on God's promises to them before or during their lives, and they were convicted that God kept all His promises. For example, Abraham did not see the conclusion of the promises of land, seed, and nation and did not know of Christ's resurrection. His hope was in the faithfulness of God, who keeps all promises. The conclusion of Hebrews 11 and Romans 4 affirm this.

> [39]*And all these, having obtained a good testimony through faith, did not receive the promise,* [40]*God having provided something better for us, that they should not be made perfect apart from us (Hebrews 11:39-40).*

> *Who, contrary to hope, in hope believed, so that he became the father of many nations, according to what was spoken, "So shall your descendants be" (Romans 4:18).*

We have the mystery of the gospel revealed to us so that we know our hope is grounded in Christ's resurrection for our salvation and that God is faithful to keep His promises. We are certain that God's grace leads to a glorious eternal life with Him in heaven, as is written in the Bible.

> *Now hope does not disappoint, because the love of God has been poured out in our hearts by the Holy Spirit who was given to us (Romans 5:5).*

> *For whatever things were written before were written for our learning, that we through the patience and comfort of the Scriptures might have hope (Romans 15:4).*

> [7]*In Him we have redemption through His blood, the forgiveness of sins, according to the riches of His grace* [8]*which He made to abound toward us in all wisdom and prudence,* [9]*having made known to us the mystery of His will, according to His good pleasure which He purposed in Himself,* [10]*that in the dispensation of the fullness of the times He might gather together in one all things in Christ, both which are in heaven and which are on earth—in Him (Ephesians 1:7-10).*

As you think about your hope, do you sing the song "The Solid Rock" by Edward Mote? The first verse sings about the basis of a Christian's hope.

> My hope is built on nothing less
> Than Jesus' blood and righteousness;
> I dare not trust the sweetest frame,
> But wholly lean on Jesus' name.

Defending Our Hope

Christians are a peculiar people, and God meant for us to be noticeably different from others. He requires Christians to be able to rationally explain the reason for their hope and faith. To do this, we must know why and what we believe! This knowledge comes from the study of the Bible in personal, group, and formal settings.

> *But sanctify the Lord God in your hearts, and always be ready to give a defense to everyone who asks you a reason for the hope that is in you, with meekness and fear (1 Peter 3:15).*

Now, most Christians will not know the complete answer to every question at any given time. It is perfectly fine to say, "I don't know right now, but let me study and get back to you." This response is acceptable as long as the Christian conducts the necessary study and the discussion continues with the questioner.

As we mature in our faith, our ability to answer questions grows. God expects this growth, and all Christians must be able to teach others and defend their hope and faith.

> *[12]For though by this time you ought to be teachers, you need someone to teach you again the first principles of the oracles of God; and you have come to need milk and not solid food. [13]For everyone who partakes only of milk is unskilled in the word of righteousness, for he is a babe. [14]But solid food belongs to those who are of full age, that is, those who by reason of use have their senses exercised to discern both good and evil (Hebrews 5:12-14).*

The Lord Is Holy

From the earliest times, God has declared Himself to be holy, which means sacred. He assures us of this fact four times in the book of Leviticus alone. For example,

> *Speak to all the congregation of the children of Israel, and say to them: "You shall be holy, for I the Lord your God am holy" (Leviticus 19:2).*

Twice in the Bible, God is described as "Holy, holy, holy"' (Isaiah 6:3 and Revelation 4:8). At the time of those writings, the repetition of a word or phrase meant superlative of the highest quality or degree. Malachi 3:6 tells us that God is the same yesterday, today, and tomorrow. Our God was the same in the Old and New Testament, has not changed today, and is our most holy God today.

The holiness of God is more than words can describe; after all, God is God. He has no equal. He is omnipresent, omnipotent, and omniscient. He is greater in every way that we can imagine. God is perfect and pure. He is awesome and majestic. He is the Great Creator. He is greater and mightier than all His creation. He is God, the great I AM.

We Must Be Holy

A hard fact for us is that God has commanded us to be holy. I, a person, am to be holy as God is holy! How can that be done? The easy answer is to be righteous as Jesus was righteous and to be obedient to God's commands.

Notice in Leviticus 19 God declared Himself to be holy and commanded the Israelites to be holy; then the rest of the chapter told the Israelites how to be holy. The following verses tell them to honor parents and sabbaths; have concern for the poor, respect for the old, and love for their neighbors and the alien; have justice in courts and just measures and weights; be honest; prohibit idolatry, pagan practices, sacred prostitution, and necromancy; and described other duties for treatment of others and plant/animal husbandry. God expected the Israelites to be holy and told them how.

Just as the Israelites were told how to be holy in the Old Testament, we Christians are told how to be holy in the New Testament. God has ordered us to be holy by living according to His righteousness through obedience to His commands.

> [1]*I beseech you therefore, brethren, by the mercies of God, that you present your bodies a living sacrifice, holy, acceptable to God, which is your reasonable service.* [2]*And do not be conformed to this world, but be transformed by the renewing of your mind, that you may prove what is that good and acceptable and perfect will of God (Romans 12:1-2).*

> [16]*Do you not know that you are the temple of God and that the Spirit of God dwells in you?* [17]*If anyone defiles the temple of God, God will destroy him. For the temple of God is holy, which temple you are (1 Corinthians 3:16-17).*

We know how to live righteously and obediently by reading and studying our Bibles. We have the four gospels to learn how Jesus lived righteously; all the New Testament to learn how a Christian lives righteously; and the Old Testament to learn God's character and life lessons. We can be holy because God wants us to be holy. He would never command us to do or be anything impossible to do, because His grace always supports us in this task whenever we come up short. We cannot be perfect in our obedience, but God's grace covers our shortcomings.

> *Who has saved us and called us with a holy calling, not according to our works, but according to His own purpose and grace which was given to us in Christ Jesus before time began (2 Timothy 1:9).*

> *And God is able to make all grace abound toward you, that you, always hav-*

ing all sufficiency in all things, may have an abundance for every good work (2 Corinthians 9:8).

Character and Actions of a Holy Person Living with Hope

The Epistle of Colossians describes how Jesus is the basis for all Christians' hope. However, Colossians 3 has descriptions of how Christians live. The following verses concisely portray a Christian's character and lifestyle. Today, our holiness has these same qualities: God's expectations.

[12]Therefore, as the elect of God, holy and beloved, put on tender mercies, kind-
ness, humility, meekness, longsuffering; [13]bearing with one another, and forgiving
one another, if anyone has a complaint against another; even as Christ forgave
you, so you also must do. [14]But above all these things put on love, which is the
bond of perfection. [15]And let the peace of God rule in your hearts, to which also
you were called in one body; and be thankful. [16]Let the word of Christ dwell in you
richly in all wisdom, teaching and admonishing one another in psalms and hymns
and spiritual songs, singing with grace in your hearts to the Lord. [17]And whatever
you do in word or deed, do all in the name of the Lord Jesus, giving thanks to God
the Father through Him (Colossians 3: 12-17).

Summary

Our hope of Christ's resurrection and heaven sustains us throughout our lives. This hope brings us joy, peace, and perseverance in good and bad times. Our hope requires us to be righteous, as Jesus was righteous and holy, as God is holy.

Discussion Questions

1. How does wearing the name of Christ affect how you live or your influence on others?

2. How would you define hope?

3. What do you think is Christian hope(s)?

4. What other examples of hope do you find in the Bible?

5. How can others see your hope?

6. Why is it important to be able to defend your hope?

7. How would you define holy?

8. How is God holy?

9. How can we be holy if holiness is of God?

10. How would you respond to someone accusing you of acting holy? Can this be a bad accusation?

11. How does a holy person act?

Job Requirement # 13

Flexibility to Perform Additional Responsibilities and Duties as Assigned in Alignment with Faith and Mission

In this lesson book, we have covered loving God and your neighbor, believing the Bible is God's word, being baptized, worshipping with the assembly and by yourself, performing good works, teaching, living peaceably and contentedly, controlling your speech, discerning, judging, and keeping yourself holy. Do we have other duties? Of course, we do! Christianity is a way of life. Lessons in this book are only the beginning of this life. As we grow in our years, we must grow as Christians, and our other duties become more numerous.

Christianity is an active faith. Going through the motions and checking the boxes on a requirements sheet does not get us into heaven. It does not matter how hard we work in God's kingdom; we cannot earn our way into heaven. God's grace and a pure heart are the final requirements. Christians have many liberties in their faith, and each person has a different walk with God, making their "other duties as assigned" different. A few possibilities for these other duties are discussed below.

If You Love Me, Keep My Commandments

Recently, on social media, this author saw a meme listing 20 verses saying, *"If you love Me, keep My commandments."* These verses were spread from Exodus to 2nd John. For example, Joshua told the Reubenites, Gadites, and half the tribe of Manasseh to love God and keep His commandments. These tribes were returning to their homes in the land they had conquered in eastern Canaan. Joshua praised them for staying and fighting to conquer the Promised Land. However, he knew that these tribes would be separated from the rest by the Jordan River and could easily slide away from God. Joshua directed,

> *But take careful heed to do the commandment and the law which Moses the servant of the Lord commanded you, to love the Lord your God, to walk in all His ways, to keep His commandments, to hold fast to Him, and to serve Him with all your heart and with all your soul" (Joshua 22:5).*

Similarly, Jesus charged His apostles, *"If you love Me, keep My commandments"* (John 14:15). This order was part of Jesus' preparation of the apostles for His coming crucifixion. His apostles did not understand all of His commandments that night, but this commandment was clear. Our obedience to Christ's commandments shows our love of Jesus. *"If you love Me, keep My commandments"* is clearly understandable to us today.

Do Good to Please God

Finding ways to help others is commanded by God. We must recognize our opportunities and act on them! Sometimes, the need is simple and easily completed. Sometimes, the good deed requires a sacrifice from us. God expects us to share with one another as the early Christians did. Galatians 6:10 tells us to do good to all, especially to those who are of the household of faith. Yes, we must take care of brethren, but care for other people too.

> *Therefore, as we have opportunity, let us do good to all, especially to those who are of the household of faith (Galatians 6:10).*

The NT tells Christians to work in the kingdom and do good deeds for others. Today, many people perform charitable works and donate money to good causes which are good deeds. The Bible directly mentions some of these causes as good deeds and infers many others are good deeds. This discussion of our good and charitable deeds in this lesson is to consider why we do them. Donating money to a good cause is great, as is working directly for a charity or a needy person. However, God wants us to work in His kingdom for His glory, not our glory. If the reason we work for or donate to a charity is recognition in our community, we have already received our reward.

> *"Take heed that you do not do your charitable deeds before men, to be seen by them. Otherwise you have no reward from your Father in heaven (Matthew 6:1).*

> *And if you do good to those who do good to you, what credit is that to you? For even sinners do the same (Luke 6:33).*

Working in God's kingdom is His commandment, and we must all do what we can. Each individual has different abilities and resources, so we work differently in the kingdom. However, there is no excuse for doing nothing because you think your work is less than someone else's.

> *Therefore, to him who knows to do good and does not do it, to him it is sin (James 4:17).*

Glorify God

The Bible does not say, "Do what makes you happy." It says to do what glorifies God, for you belong to Him. Often, people justify their actions by saying God wants them to be happy. Was John the Baptist happy when Herod cut off his head? Was Steven happy when the Sanhedrin Council stoned him to death? Both would have chosen something else if their goal was to be happy. A Christian's goal is to glorify God in the way that they think and live! The NT says we are happy when we do not approve of something that God has condemned.

> *For you were bought at a price; therefore glorify God in your body and in your spirit, which are God's (1 Corinthians 6:20).*

Do you have faith? Have it to yourself before God. Happy is he who does not condemn himself in what he approves (Romans 14:22).

Find Joy

Joy is important in the life of a Christian. Joy is an enduring pleasure, satisfaction, or contentment that comes from within rather than external circumstances. Christian joy is based on faith in Jesus and living as He has commanded. First-century Christians reveled in their joy, whether in good and hard times. They found joy in their faith and in the trials they faced, serving as Christian examples to others.

And being confident of this, I know that I shall remain and continue with you all for your progress and joy of faith (Philippians 1:25).

[10]that you may walk worthy of the Lord, fully pleasing Him, being fruitful in every good work and increasing in the knowledge of God; [11]strengthened with all might, according to His glorious power, for all patience and longsuffering with joy (Colossians 1:10-11).

[6]And you became followers of us and of the Lord, having received the word in much affliction, with joy of the Holy Spirit, [7]so that you became examples to all in Macedonia and Achaia who believe (1 Thessalonians 1:6-7).

Finding joy in good times is easier than when life's trials have found us. Financial or health issues can dull or squash our joy in Jesus. We must persevere in our faith, knowing He is with us until the end, even if our end is physical death, as we will receive our reward of salvation and eternal life. James 1:2 encourages us during our hard times, *"My brethren, count it all joy when you fall into various trials."*

Jesus did not promise that being a Christian would be easy, but has promised He will be with us. Our joy is in that promise.

Give Up Our Idols

In our contemporary time, people do not realize that idols can be part of our modern lives. We think stone statues of ancient gods are more of a museum piece or archeological wonder than a religious focus. Don't let the primeval stone image fool you. We can have idols today, just as those idols of olden ages. These are idols in our hearts and are anything or anyone we prioritize over God. They can be wealth, fame, ballgames, yard work, jobs, sex, celebrities, family, or a convenient life. Modern idols are often common life elements, but slowly grow in priority until they have surpassed God in our lives. These sneaky, modern idols can cause us to be separated from God before we realize anything has happened.

God told Ezekiel about these idols in Ezekiel 14:3, *"Son of man, these men have set up their idols in their hearts, and put before them that which causes them to stumble*

.. *iniquity."* He warned Ezekiel that He would turn away from anyone who prioritized anything over Him and did not repent. *"I will set My face against that man and make him a sign and a proverb, and I will cut him off from the midst of My people. Then you shall know that I am the LORD" (Ezekiel 14:8).*

Recognize the Need for God's Mercy and Grace

We all need God's mercy and grace, as we cannot earn our way into heaven. Nothing we have or do will buy an entrance ticket. We have all sinned, and that separates us from God and keeps us from those pearly gates. For God is sinless and cannot tolerate sin. However, He loves us and wants to save us from eternal separation, and He sent Jesus for the propitiation of our sins.

> *23for all have sinned and fall short of the glory of God, 24being justified freely by His grace through the redemption that is in Christ Jesus (Romans 3:24).*

> *4But God, who is rich in mercy, because of His great love with which He loved us, 5even when we were dead in trespasses, made us alive together with Christ (by grace you have been saved) (Ephesians 2:4-5).*

God's mercy and grace blot out sin for those obedient Christians whose imperfections were washed away through baptism and who lived righteous lives. We don't earn our salvation, even as the most obedient Christians, but need His mercy and grace to be perfect and live with Him eternally.

> *11For the grace of God that brings salvation has appeared to all men, 12teaching us that, denying ungodliness and worldly lusts, we should live soberly, righteously, and godly in the present age (Titus 2:11-12).*

> *Not by works of righteousness which we have done, but according to His mercy He saved us, through the washing of regeneration and renewing of the Holy Spirit (Titus 3:5).*

Love Yourself

This author realized the need to add this "duty" because of a mainstream television show! The main character was a policeman who had a terrible childhood and thought himself worthless. He only realized his value and learned to love himself after someone taught him about God and how God commanded Christians to love themselves. It seems a simple idea, but some Christians do not like themselves for their misdeeds in the past or the attitudes of others toward them.

> *For all the law is fulfilled in one word, even in this: "You shall love your neighbor as yourself" (Galatians 5:14).*

Verses stating "love others as yourself" are often used to teach us to do good for others. However, consider the last phrase of this verse—"as yourself." We must love and value ourselves! God values and loves us and expects His children to recognize their worth to Him.

Encourage One Another

Christians are to encourage and teach one another by supporting and helping their brethren with their spiritual growth and perseverance. Our actions and words should guide and support another's walk with Christ.

> *Therefore comfort each other and edify one another, just as you also are doing (1 Thessalonians 5:11).*

Sometimes, we support our brethren by not doing something that is a liberty. Romans 14 teaches us about carefully using our liberties with weaker Christians. This particular example involved eating meat offered in markets that had first been offered to idols. To weaker Christians, it was a sin to eat that meat. Until they had grown in their faith, it was a sin. Other Christians were not to cause them to stumble by encouraging the eating of the offered meat, and to refrain from eating the meat with those Christians.

Paul wrote this short list of actions to encourage others in his exhortation found at the end of 1 Thessalonians.

> *12And we urge you, brethren, to recognize those who labor among you, and are*
> *over you in the Lord and admonish you, 13and to esteem them very highly in*
> *love for their work's sake. Be at peace among yourselves. 14Now we exhort you,*
> *brethren, warn those who are unruly, comfort the fainthearted, uphold the weak,*
> *be patient with all. 15See that no one renders evil for evil to anyone, but always*
> *pursue what is good both for yourselves and for all. 16Rejoice always, 17pray with-*
> *out ceasing, 18in everything give thanks; for this is the will of God in Christ Jesus*
> *for you. 19Do not quench the Spirit. 20Do not despise prophecies. 21Test all things;*
> *hold fast what is good. 22Abstain from every form of evil (1 Thessalonians 5:12-22).*

Encouragement is vital for all Christians, even Paul. For example, the Philippian church supported Paul financially when no other church did (Philippians 4:15). Even though Demas, Alexander, and others had disappointed or harmed Paul, Mark, Luke, and Tychicus served with him (2 Timothy 4:9-16). Encouragement is essential for all as we finish our race on earth.

Summary

This lesson book is not an exhaustive list of all things a Christian should do, as no book written by a person can do that. Only God's inspired book, the Bible, can tell us all and reveal the mysteries of the gospel.

Discussion Questions

1. Why is the walk with God different for each Christian?

2. How is our love for Jesus shown in obedience?

3. Can Christians limit good deeds to those of the household of faith? When would this be appropriate, and when would it not?

4. If you are publically recognized for doing good deeds, were they done for God's glory?

5. What applications can be made from Romans 14:22 in today's culture about pursuing happiness?

6. How do we know if we have joy in Jesus?

7. How can idols in our hearts become more important to us than Jesus? How can we protect ourselves from these idols?

8. How do we love ourselves as Christians?

9. How can we be an encouragement to others?

10. Why can 'other duties as assigned' be different for each Christian?

Submitting Your Resume

We search for job postings whenever we need an earthly job. First, we read the posting and compare our experience, education, skills and abilities to the posted qualifications. Before applying, we consider our resume to ensure it highlights our applicable qualifications. God has posted a job, also. He has called mankind to be His followers before time and wants everyone to find salvation through Christ.

> *[9]Who has saved us and called us with a holy calling, not according to our works, but according to His own purpose and grace which was given to us in Christ Jesus before time began, [10]but has now been revealed by the appearing of our Savior Jesus Christ, who has abolished death and brought life and immortality to light through the gospel (2 Timothy 1:9-10).*

> *[1]I, therefore, the prisoner of the Lord, beseech you to walk worthy of the calling with which you were called, [2]with all lowliness and gentleness, with longsuffering, bearing with one another in love, [3]endeavoring to keep the unity of the Spirit in the bond of peace. [4]There is one body and one Spirit, just as you were called in one hope of your calling; [5]one Lord, one faith, one baptism; [6]one God and Father of all, who is above all, and through all, and in you all (Ephesians 4:1-6).*

The posting calls us to be in the one body, one Spirit, one hope, one Lord, one faith, and one baptism. God has made the job posting; we must have the qualifications. However, none of us can ever fulfill all the qualifications of a Christian, as being sinless is the minimum requirement to live eternally in heaven.

> *[23]For all have sinned and fall short of the glory of God, [24]being justified freely by His grace through the redemption that is in Christ Jesus (Romans 3:23-24).*

God cannot tolerate sin, and all of us have sinned. However, with His mercy and grace, God forgives and forgets our sins to allow us this sinless quality.

> *[12]Giving thanks to the Father who has qualified us to be partakers of the inheritance of the saints in the light. [13]He has delivered us from the power of darkness and conveyed us into the kingdom of the Son of His love, [14]in whom we have redemption through His blood, the forgiveness of sin. (Colossians 1:12-14).*

So, work on those qualifications and apply for heaven! God welcomes all faithful followers who strive to be workers in His kingdom.

Made in the USA
Las Vegas, NV
01 March 2026

42902138R00063